The Wealth of
Families

The Wealth of
Families

Building, Preserving,
and Transferring Wealth

Jack Ellis, CPA, JD

Dove
Publishers

Bladensburg, MD

The Wealth of Families
Published by
Inscript Books
a division of Dove Christian Publishers
P.O. Box 611
Bladensburg, MD 20710-0611
www.dovechristianpublishers.com

ISBN: 978-1-7359529-9-4
Library of Congress Catalog No. 2021938017

Published in the United States of America
25 24 23 22 21 20 1 2 3 4 5

Dedication

I would be remiss if I did not first mention the ultimate source of all wisdom: God and His Word, the Bible. It has always been my teacher and friend and inspiration. It has been called the Bottomless Book. I first heard that reference from one of my dearest mentors, Kevin Lister. He was able to impart the wisdom of the Bible in a way that resonated with my Spirit and made it easily accessible when I needed it in a particular situation. I also fondly remember Bill Klinger, a mentor who saw my potential for financial ministry and gently guided me in that direction.

I will always be thankful for our dear neighbors, Miriam and Larry. They set us on the road to salvation and discipled us in the things of the Lord. They have been used greatly to advance God's kingdom and increase the number of saints going into the kingdom.

Pastor Dave M. was also a source of great inspiration early on in my Christian walk. He had the innate ability and wisdom to get you to expand your own abilities and wisdom and maximize your service to God. He encouraged me to use my musical abilities in the youth group in our church. Also, he allowed me to teach the youth biblical financial concepts, which sharpened my abilities in this area. He greatly encouraged and motivated all who served with him.

Further, Pastor Dave H. has had an enormous impact on my spiritual maturity. His explanation of the word of God has helped me increase my maturity as I walk through this life. I believe he has positively impacted my family members as well, many of whom sit under his teaching. He not only talks the talk, but he walks the walk. And as many have said, "It's not what's taught, it's what's caught." As the Bible teaches, you need to get out from under the "what's in it for me" attitude and start to treat others better than yourself. In writing this book, that's what I'm striving for—to benefit others by my counsel, learning what I learned from the Bible, both my successes and failures. Often, as is said, we learn a lot more from our failures. The only thing I am striving to accomplish is to advance God's kingdom by training fellow strugglers to get their financial house in order. In my life, I have found that when you honor God with your finances, many blessings result.

I especially want to dedicate this work to those family members who were my first teachers: my Mom and Dad. My Dad showed me how to confront a challenge and prize a son. Mom taught me the loyalty and faith of a tireless worker who cared and enjoyed her family and loved her Lord.

Also, to my most influential teacher, my beloved wife and life partner, Debi. She has always been a wonder to me, a tireless servant whose energy, compassion, and caring for others is an inspiration. Her uncanny spiritual awareness and insight are sometimes baffling to me and always rooted in caring for others better than herself.

And to my ongoing teachers; my three sons (sounds like a TV show). Michael, who is teaching me how to counsel and help the less fortunate. Philip, who is teaching me to be enthusiastic and enjoy life and fully utilize our God-given brilliance. And to Matthew, who is teaching me that I can accomplish any task through tireless effort and perseverance.

Also, to my three daughters-in-law, Jen, Katie, and Maria. They are all stay-at-home moms, having left their intended careers to care full-time for their families. What a blessing for our sons. They are teaching me sacrifice and devotion to family.

Finally, to my future teachers; my thirteen grandchildren (Trent, Sienna, Austin, Zac, Dean, Summer, Savanah, Selena, Philip, Andrew, Samantha, Ezra, and Elijah). I am enjoying what they are teaching me today and looking forward to all that they will be teaching me in the future. And a special thank you to Summer, Savanah, and Selena, who did all the artwork in the book. Very creative.

Contents

Introduction

Why I am writing this book? Hopefully to pass on the wisdom I have obtained about finances and other related topics while living on this earth. Obviously, since I am purporting to pass on the wisdom I have acquired, I should let you know my background and give you insight into how I acquired that wisdom. I would like to say that I got my wisdom from my parents and college and law school and now am fully wised up and will pass that stunning insight on to my readers and everything will be great for you going forward. But that would be far from the truth. Like many of you, I received some very valuable lessons from my parents. But most of those lessons were taught from the perspective of learning what *not* to do. My parents did teach me the value of having a job and working hard. But handling money and acquiring wealth was not one of their strong suits. So, you would then surmise that my advanced education gave me my finance skills. NO. My advanced education gave me a lot of debt and a degree, and it helped me get interviews to get a job. But, I didn't get any financial skills until I started going to church and studying the Bible.

I was amazed that Jesus had plenty to say about money and finances. Probably because He knew we would listen when He talked about money. A well-known Christian financial teacher, Larry Burkett, stated that over two-thirds of the parables of Jesus deal with money and finances. In fact, many of the financial concepts we use today in business and finance come from the teachings in the Bible. For example, a cornerstone of investing, diversification, comes from the Bible. Another thing that amazed me was that many of the financial principles taught in the Bible were very familiar and easy to apply. I promise to get into more detail about these principles in the later chapters.

Next, I want to talk about the financial tips that I've learned over the past 60 years of my time on this earth. I have spent a lot of time counseling individuals and couples regarding financial problems they have encountered. Through these counseling sessions, I have learned a great deal about people and how they process advice and information about their financial lives. In a sense, they have been my guinea pigs in finding out what works and what doesn't work and what people are actually willing to implement in their lives to change their financial destiny.

The main thing I have realized is that people will not implement advice that is too complicated or too burdensome. Therefore, throughout this book, I will try to make my advice straightforward and simple to implement while also striving for effective outcomes.

I will leave you with the simple truths of a well-known preacher, John Wesley. He had three simple rules for managing money: earn all you can, save all you can, and give all you can. His estate planning was also simple. He stated that if I die with more than 100 pounds (less than $150) in my estate, I will consider myself a failure. His plan was to distribute all his wealth during his lifetime. Wise words to ponder.

Let's summarize some of the topics that I will discuss in this book. First, how do you build wealth? To build wealth, one must acquire wealth, and to acquire wealth one must get a job or create a job by starting a business. So, job number one is to get educated and get a job. Once some money is coming in, you need to simply save more than you spend and have a surplus to build wealth. We will set up a budget to track our expenses and ensure a surplus.

Next, we will talk about preserving wealth while working and after you retire. To preserve wealth, we need to have and maintain a budget and stick to the spending listed in the budget. This will ensure that we will acquire and preserve wealth since we will be following the budget and spending less than we earn. We need to set goals and implement financial strategies to reach those goals.

Once we have preserved wealth, we need to talk about teaching financial principles to our loved ones. This is an important concept since we have a duty to pass on the wisdom we have learned to our children. With this education, we are confident that our children will be self-sufficient and able to preserve their own wealth. At the very least we have fulfilled our duty to them in passing on our wisdom whether they apply that wisdom to their lives or not.

Next, we need to talk about the how, when, and why to pass your wealth on to your families and charities. This is a very important subject and is really the reason why I decided to write this book. Once I retired and had a significant sum in my 401k, I searched to find guidance on how best to transfer this wealth to my loved ones and charities. There was very little guidance out there to help me and give me wisdom on the subject. Therefore, I decided to write this book and to walk through the steps I took to obtain wisdom on how to transfer wealth. Hopefully, this book will help others to craft a plan to transfer their wealth in a way that honors God and sustains their families.

Of course, before you decide to transfer wealth you need to understand your financial position and your needs so that you don't become a burden on your family while trying to help them. Therefore, I will take great pains in this book to ensure you ascertain your needs carefully, and then whatever is left over can be transferred with confidence to the next generation. We will look at the conventional wisdom regarding how to pass on wealth to your family. We will then compare that wisdom to my suggestions in this book. Once having looked at and compared my methods with the conventional ones, we will discuss the pros and cons of each approach and let you decide for yourself which one is right.

I need to warn you that most of the wisdom I have obtained regarding financial topics comes from the Bible. I don't claim to have any wisdom of my own but freely admit that the source of wisdom is the Bible. For those of you who have a more secular approach, I believe that this book will still be of use to you. Even in the secular arena, many business ideas originated from the Bible, whether you are aware of this fact or not. Therefore, I believe the suggestions in this book will be useful to you in your search for financial freedom. I also can say with confidence that from my financial counseling experience, these principles, if applied diligently, will work. The folks that I have counseled have become independent and debt-free, including the home mortgage, and have accumulated significant wealth following these time-tested principles. Of course, the key to the success of any method is to follow the principles given and to diligently apply those principles to the best of your ability.

I also want to explain what this book is not. It will not give you a detailed path on how to decide what job you should take based on your skill set. That is obviously beyond the scope of this book. While this is an important subject, you need to consult other more qualified authors and sources to tackle this involved topic. The important point is that you should develop a solid work ethic, and this will lead you to a job which will provide a steady income. This is the first step towards building wealth. It is also important to carefully ascertain your skill set and find the job that best utilizes your innate, natural skills. That way, you will maximize your enjoyment and income potential in your chosen profession.

Of course, this book will talk about the importance of budgeting. It will also talk about setting up a budget, how to save, and will touch on investment ideas. However, there are many books that discuss these subjects in detail. I will give my ideas on these topics. But my main emphasis is on procedures to simplify the implementation of a budget. I have found in my counseling sessions that procedure is just as important as the principles. Since even though the principles are grasped by a student, if the procedure to apply the principles is too complicated, they won't be followed very long or at all. So, I will stress simplicity at the risk of perfection so that you will eventually follow these principles and, once adopted, you will see positive results.

Similarly, with investing, most people would rather have experts do this for them. I will give you some simple alternatives that will save you investment fees, which can add up to a significant savings over time. However, for some people, having an expert handle investments may be a better choice for peace of mind. In all cases, I will lay out the pros and cons and let you decide.

The main point of this book is to determine how to pass on the wealth you have accumulated over many years. I suspect that many of us are in the same boat. We have saved for retirement for 30 or 40 years. We have a significant sum of money in our retirement funds, some in a traditional individual retirement account (IRA) and some in a Roth IRA. We have learned to be frugal and thus have not needed the money in our IRAs. So, the question is, how do we transfer this wealth to the next generation? Or, do we transfer it at all? This is the question that has concerned me. Finding there is very little guidance out there has caused me to write this book.

Now some of you may be thinking, *I never really had a budget, I have some wealth but have not accumulated very much. I didn't really think too much about my finances over the years. Is it too late to implement these ideas?* I would encourage you not to be discouraged. It's never too late to learn new ideas and pass them on to your children and grandchildren. Even if your children are adults, they will very likely appreciate the attempt to give them new ideas, if they are good ideas and worthy of consideration. I will let you decide that. Now, if you have started late, the implementation will be different. However, it still will be of benefit to you and your heirs. It's always beneficial to assess your finances and make positive changes that will mark you as good stewards of your possessions.

Let's start on this journey of dealing positively with the wealth that God has given us and how we will handle it for future generations. I truly hope this book will help you in this journey. I am convinced the advice in this book, if followed diligently, will produce positive results for you and your family that will last many generations. And my aim is that these results will be pleasing to God and advance His kingdom.

1.
Building
Wealth

*F*irst of all, I would like to give you my credentials. Not to brag, of course, but to give you some confidence in my advice given in this book. Hopefully, you will believe I have some experience and expertise in the subject and concepts I am putting forth.

My Background

I went to college in the 1970s. Everyone was going to college at that time. And besides, my father encouraged me in this direction since the thinking at the time was that, to get ahead, you had to have the sheepskin. At my father's urging, I started out in Aeronautical Engineering. That was a rigorous undertaking. After my first year and many F's, I realized I was not engineering material. I was interested in Computer Science and that would have been a wise undertaking at the time, but the college I went to would not let me change my major to Computer Science since it had to be approved, and with my grades, it was not. Therefore, I took a liberal arts approach and changed my major to Psychology. Once I graduated, I realized you really had to have a master's degree to get any decent job in the social sciences. But since I didn't have a real interest in that discipline, I decided to go to law school.

You can probably see that I really didn't have a great idea of what I wanted to do with my life career-wise. But I did get into law school and graduate with a law degree in 1978. During law school, quite by accident, I learned I had a very good aptitude for numbers and tax law.

Most of my law school friends hated tax law, but I loved it and understood it readily. I just had a God-given natural aptitude in that subject. I was able to help them get through the mandatory tax law course, which served to repay all the help I received regarding constitutional law and torts. I decided to work with the IRS upon graduation and went to the national office in D.C. after a short stint doing tax auditing. I was involved in policy matters and drafting private letter rulings and revenue rulings and reviewing tax legislation. I also spent time in the IRS appeals office handling large corporate tax appeals.

Upon my retirement, I stayed active in tax preparation in my church and volunteered as treasurer for the church. In that capacity, I was able to help the church comply with tax laws and keep the finances in order. I became interested in financial counseling and taught many classes in financial management and budgeting. I also met with many individuals and couples to help them get out of debt, set up budgets, save and invest, and help with planning for college and retirement.

How to Build Wealth

So, here we are, how to build wealth. It's one of those concepts that is easily described, but very hard to implement. It takes great drive and discipline to put this very easy concept into practice. And in my many counseling sessions, I have seen most folks struggle to put it into practice really effectively. Most of them are often looking for a quick fix to their problem. I usually ask people how long it took them to get into debt. For some, the debt could have been as little as a few thousand dollars; for others, it could have been as large as hundreds of thousands. But many would reply that it took several years to amass the debt. Then I would tell them it was going to take that long to eliminate the debt. At that point, many fell away because they didn't have the drive to go the distance to resolve the problem. There is a minority that will put the plan into action and drive until the debt is gone. But the majority do it halfheartedly and get mixed results. Then there is another minority that will start well and get some results but will not take it all the way to complete resolution. A good analogy is the parable of the sower, which relates to those who will seek and find the Kingdom of God. This is found in Matthew 17, which you may read for your edification. I hope you will fall into the group that really has the discipline to take building wealth seriously and go the distance. You will be blessed and your family will prosper, I can assure you.

Let's look at the simple principle of building wealth. You simply must spend less than you earn and save the difference. That's how people get into debt; they don't follow this principle. You must understand what you bring in each month and strive to spend less than you bring in monthly. If you can do this, you will build wealth over time. And with the power of compounding, the amount of wealth you can accumulate is surprising. Just do a Google search on the power of compounding and you will see many examples of how this concept works in real life. The point of these examples is to focus on two principles. First, you must start saving early in your life. Second, even a small monthly amount that is saved regularly over time will grow to a small fortune.

Of course, for the undisciplined, it is much easier to spend more than you make and go into debt. It satisfies the "I want it now" thinking of today's young folks. Let me say that we all think like that, young or old. It's fun to get it now and worry about the payments later. But, believe me, I have seen the long-term results that kind of thinking will bring about. There are many shattered lives, broken relationships and marriages, and great stress and health problems associated with having too much debt. Not to mention the lost opportunity of putting the power of compounding into practice as early as possible.

When you graduate from school, you need to find a job that suits your abilities. Although beyond the scope of this book, it is important to get the right education for the job you seek, to determine where your gifts and career desires lie, and to focus on jobs that make the best use of those gifts, talents, and desires. By taking the time to examine your gifts, talents, and desires you will get a job that makes the best use of your unique talent. In this position, you will be happy, your employer will be happy, and both of you will receive the maximum benefit in terms of longevity, productivity, and compensation. Therefore, I encourage you to take all the time necessary to ensure you are properly trained and gifted for your chosen occupation. There are many resources available to help you in this area. One resource is the book, *What Color is Your Parachute?*

Once you have secured the perfect job and have maximized your income, it's time to employ the strategy of building wealth. The foremost tool to secure your wealth is the monthly budget. I know; that is a dirty word for some. When we hear the word *budget*, we think of tightening our spending, the unseen hand of restricting our wants and desires, and just the overall negative connotations the austere budget can bring. It doesn't have to be that way at all. I often tell people, "it's your budget, not an unseen hand." You approve all the spending in your budget. Once people truly understand the concept and start working with budgeting principles, they usually find it liberating. They now know where their money is actually going, they have an emergency fund saved up in case something unexpected happens, they don't feel guilty anymore when they spend, and they know they are actually starting to reach their savings goals.

Budgeting

OK, how to budget. First, we have to find a good budget worksheet. There are many out there. I like the one on Kiplinger's or Crown Financial website. It's straightforward, only one page, and it has the most common expenses people will have. That's important since you don't want to miss anything. It also lets you add rows for additional income or expense items. So, it is customizable to your situation. There are many forms out there on the internet, so you can choose one that works best for you. You're looking for something fairly simple and straightforward that is easy to follow but includes the most common expenses. The budget worksheet allows you to forecast your monthly income and expenses. It will list sources of income, mostly from your paycheck. I do not include income from investments since these monies will be plowed back into your savings to maximize the compounding effect. Then it will list all the normally occurring expenses you have every month.

At this point, I want to talk about online budget programs. *Intuit Mint* has a good one and I have noticed my bank has one as well. They are pretty sophisticated. They pull in your credit card expenses and all your income as well as everything you write checks for. From what I understand, the security is good. I am hesitant to give Mint all of my passwords, but it is necessary for a complete understanding of your spending. There is one major drawback with these programs: they do not anticipate non-monthly expense items. They are excellent at tracking your monthly spending, but they do not plan for all your expenditures and your savings for retirement, college funding, debt elimination, and other goals you have set. So, while they are helpful, they really do not do the job of a comprehensive budget.

Now you need to fill out the budget form. Get out your pay stubs, checkbook, bank statements, and credit card statements and start filling out the form. List all your income from your jobs and any other non-job income you may have. Then decide what you want to give to your church and how much you want to save and invest. After that, whatever is left over is used for your expenses. You need to carefully look at your checkbook and ensure you have included all your expenses. If you are not sure what amount to put in for an expense item, your checkbook will give you clues. You can also consult the internet as there are many recommended guidelines that list what % of your total monthly net spendable income should be allocated for each expense item. Also, look for ATM withdrawals or other cash expenditures to ensure to include those cash expenses. Now, the fun part of a budget is that you get to decide what you give to the church and how much you can save for investment. Also, you can decide what your expenses will amount to since you can control most aspects of your spending. That's where the discipline will come in. How bad do you want this to work? How bad do you want to be debt-free and to control your spending instead of it controlling you? And how bad do you want your financial future to be bright rather than a source of stress and disappointment? As you do the mundane work of filling out the budget form, think about these thoughts.

Many times, as I counseled people on filling out their budget, I saw their excitement as they realized they were finally controlling their own financial future. This is usually a surprise since most people think of budgeting as boring and restricting their spending. And we don't like to be restricted. But people who are in debt and stressed out are very happy to get rid of that stress, and budgeting is the effective tool they need to get started. Invariably, the first time you fill out the budget form (yes, you will make many drafts before it is perfected), you will probably have too many expenses and not enough income. Then you will have to perform surgery to get your expenses down to the point where your income matches your expenses and savings goals. That is the difficult part and that's where the budget counselor can provide insight on ways to reduce your expenses to achieve your important long-term goals.

For example, let's say a couple is filling out their budget. They really don't know what to put down for entertainment/recreation, so they look at their past vacations and dining out and put down $400 per month. The counselor knows that this is too high and will throw the budget out of whack. He will suggest a lower number that is in line with recommended guidelines for this line item. He might suggest a figure around $200. Then, the couple must make a decision. Do they want to maintain this item and cut some other items, or revise their vacation habits and use the recommended number?

These are the kinds of decisions you will have to make as you adjust your budget expense items to get them in line with your income. Once you thoughtfully balance your budget to match income and expenses, you are well on your way to financial freedom.

In the end, it's your budget and your future you are deciding on. You have to decide how to balance short-term spending versus long-term savings and investment goals. It's the wise steward who sacrifices short-term gratification for the long-term good of his family.

Speaking of family, I should discuss who will be filling out the budget form, allocating the numbers, and managing the budget as it is implemented. That person would be the both of you if you have a spouse; otherwise, enlist a trusted friend who knows you and your spending habits and has a flair for numbers. Both of you must participate in your financial future. Usually, one of you is good with numbers and will keep the checkbook balanced and doesn't mind managing a budget. That person will be the best one for doing the hands-on work. But both of you must share in the decision-making of budgeting and spending. I have counseled in situations where one person desperately wants to get spending under control with a budget and the other person could care less. This always ends in disaster. You and your spouse got your financial future out of control and you both must agree to get it back together. Otherwise, one person is handling all the stress and the other one is along for the free ride. It never works. I can explain all the benefits of budgeting and being debt-free, but until the holdout wants to truly participate, it will never come to fruition.

OK, now you have the budget worksheet completed and agreed upon by your loved ones. Ensure you include your spouse, so everyone who has a stake in your financial future is on board. You know how much income you have and you have allocated it to your giving, savings, investments, and all your monthly expenses. You worked hard to balance your income with your expenses and savings. The budget is a tool and the first step to getting us to our goal. We now have to implement the budget into our daily living and spending so that we meet our goals in reality. Otherwise, making the budget is a useless exercise to make us feel good without producing any results.

Here we go. At this point, I will say that it's important to implement the budget in a simple and effective way. I have encountered some experts whose implementation is so complicated and daunting that no average person will ever implement the budget. This is a tragedy because once you have the written budget and figure out how to implement it, that is when you are on the road to building wealth. I have formulated a method that involves setting up most of your expenses on a monthly basis (budget plan). Once that is done, you determine which monthly expenses are fixed and which ones are variable. Then, you take the monthly equivalent of your non-monthly expenses and put that into a savings account. After that, you simply monitor your checkbook balance to ensure you are staying on track.

Let me explain how this will work in practice with some numbers. Here is the completed monthly budget worksheet for Bob and Barb:

Monthly Budget

Monthly Income

Gross monthly income	$6,000
Salary	$6,000
Interest	
Other inc.	
Less	
Giving	($500)
Taxes & other withholds	($1,000)
Net Spendable Income	**$4,500**

Monthly Living Expenses

Housing	$1,985
Mortgage	$1,500
Insurance	
Prop taxes	
Electric *	$65
Gas *	$65
Water *	$20
Garbage *	$40
Telephone	$70
Maintenance (2)	$125

TV & Internet	$100
Food (1)	$550
Transportation	$760
Payments	
Gas & Oil (1)	$100
Auto Insurance *	$250
License (2)	$10
Repair/replace (2)	$400
Insurance	$40
Life *	$40
Health	
Other	
Debts	$0
Entertain/Recreation	$210
Eating out (1)	$60
Activities	
Vacation (2)	$150
Pets	
Other	
Clothing (2)	$75
Savings	$100
Medical	$100
Doctor (2)	$50
Dentist (2)	$50
Drugs	
Miscellaneous	$150
Toiletries	
Cleaning	
Gifts	
Cash	$150
Other	
Investments	$500

School/Child care	$30
Tuition	
Materials (2)	$30
Transport.	
Daycare	
Total Living Expenses	**$4,500**
Surplus or Deficit	$0

(1) = monthly variable expense, (2) = non-monthly to savings * = on budget plan

As you can see, they have a good amount of income, around $72,000. But, for a family of 4, that is about the average income in the good old USA in 2020. No matter the income level, this method will work. I have counseled folks with incomes of $30,000 and over $150,000, and everyone in-between. Discipline in sticking with the plan will make the difference. I have tried to think of the normal expenses this family will have, including giving to the church and internet expenses, a necessity these days. I have also allowed generous amounts for home and car maintenance and replacement, as well as savings and investment. I have assumed Bob's company pays for his health care plan. Otherwise, most of the family upkeep is on them.

Let's talk a minute about home and car maintenance expenses. These are important areas to anticipate and budget since they are usually budget busters. They are typically not thought about and can wreak havoc on the budget. And that's precisely why we try to anticipate these variable expenses in advance so that when they inevitably occur, you will not be in a panic about how to pay them. Here is what normally happens when an unexpected home or car repair is needed. The family has not budgeted for them, and so they use their credit card to pay for them. However, since they are not on a budget and are not controlling their spending, the credit card bill cannot be paid off in full the next month. So, they put the minimum payment on the card and incur very high interest charges, in the range of 14 to 21%. This cycle repeats itself over a few years and without warning, the couple has credit card debt of $50,000 or more. That is the situation we are trying to avoid. Unfortunately, many times the couples I have counseled are already in this situation, stressed out and desperately needing an escape route.

Finally, I have assumed there is no outstanding debt for the family except for the home mortgage. They are using a debit card or, if using credit, the full balance is paid off each month. Note that even if there is debt, the budget is very capable of handling this problem. One of the main benefits of having a budget is to rein in spending so that you can eventually pay off all debt. Although beyond the scope of this book, the tried and true method of paying off all debt is using the debt snowball. In this method, you apportion a set amount in your budget for all debt payoffs. (You must also put an amount in your budget to meet all minimum payments on your debts.) Let's say that amount is $300 per month. And let's say you have 5 debts; the lowest payoff balance is $210 and the highest is $3,200. You take the $300 every month and apply it to the lowest payoff debt until that is paid off and work your way up to the highest payoff debt. I have seen this method work amazingly well, and it's fun to see the encouragement and excitement as people start seeing their debts melt away and the associated stress lifted.

Note that I have labeled some of the expense items with an asterisk, a number 1 or a number 2. The asterisk expenses are variable expenses such as utilities or insurance that the company allows Bob to set up on a monthly budget plan. I encourage folks to do this as much as possible since it allows for easier planning when budgeting. The expenses labeled 1 are incurred every month but are variable and not fixed amounts every month. These expenses cause some trouble with the budget and must be watched more carefully. Likewise, the expenses marked 2 are not incurred every month and must be totaled and transferred to a savings account to ensure there is enough money set aside from the monthly budget to pay those expenses when they become due. The remaining expenses are incurred monthly and are fixed in amount. Those are the least bothersome since they come up every month and we know the exact amount to budget.

Implementing the Budget

So, let's go about implementing this well-planned and balanced budget. The first thing we must do is to ensure we can monitor the checking account very closely. This is the key to keeping the budget and staying on track. So, you need to get on your bank's website and register for online banking. It's then very easy to monitor your balance and track your expenses and payments. You will want to direct deposit your income into your checking account. Remember, your net pay will be deposited into your account. In Bob's case, this is $5,000. I recommend you have all your expenses, or as many as possible, set up on auto-pay. This way you will never miss a payment and you will avoid those nasty late fees.

I also would use a debit card rather than a credit card. With a debit card, your daily expenditures are tracked in real-time with deductions from your checking account. Because of the 30-day float with credit cards, your expenditures in one month will show up in the next month. This can wreak havoc on the budget. It's also much easier to overspend with a credit card as opposed to using cash or a debit card. Why do you think the credit card companies offer you those points and cashback deals? Do you think they are just nice people? Statistically, they know that most people will overspend, on average, 10 to 15% more when using credit. If you really want to use a credit card, my suggestion is to use the debit card until you are really on track with your budget; at least six months to a year. Then, you can try the credit card since your spending habits should be ingrained by this time.

The next thing we must do is to compute the total of expenses labeled 2 and put that amount into a savings account. With the advent of online banking, it's very easy to transfer funds from checking into other accounts; especially when those accounts are within the same bank. So, in our example, we have eight expense items labeled 2. These eight items total $890. So, every month, we will transfer that $890 into the savings account. We also have $100 in our budget for savings. So that amount will also be transferred to the savings account every month, for a total of $990. You could have your bank automatically transfer that amount on a date of your choosing every month. That way, everything is done automatically so nothing is forgotten or left out. Likewise, we have $500 for investments in the budget. You could instruct your broker or mutual fund company to transfer that amount from your bank automatically.

At this point, you might be wondering, why do you put an extra $100 in the savings account if all expenses are covered? It's nice to have a cushion since most of the expenses going into the savings account are variable expenses that vary from month to month. Even before we start budgeting, I encourage folks to have $500 to $1,000 extra in the checking account so there is no problem with overdrafts on your checking account if some higher than normal variable expense is paid out. With these extra safeguards, the budget should run smoothly. Once these steps are undertaken, you can let your budget run on its own and simply track your checking account balance very carefully. Every few days is recommended.

There are a couple of additional items I should mention. You should be aware anytime an expenditure is made for one of the eight expense items labeled 2. Since these amounts have been deposited into your savings account, anytime one of these expenses is paid out of your checking account, that amount must be transferred from savings back into your checking. I suggest having these eight expense items listed on a separate sheet of paper to have for handy reference anytime you examine your checkbook balance and review your expenditures.

The other item is cash. Note that we have put $150 into the budget for cash. This is for Bob and Barb to withdraw using their ATM cards for their personal use. We thought of everything!

Getting back to monitoring your checkbook; you should examine your expenditures carefully each time you view your balance. These expenditures should be compared with your budget worksheet. That way, if any expense item is getting out of hand, you will be able to rein in it before the month is out and/or you have exceeded your balance. You might ask, "what if my balance is running very low and there are several days left in the month or even a week?" Well, in that case, you stop spending and wait until next month. That is the discipline that makes your budget work. You will be happy you did. If you are exceeding your balance regularly, then you must investigate your expenses to see where you are overspending. At that point, you have two choices. You either rein in the spending for that budget account item or you change your budget by raising the offensive item in your budget, but you must also lower some other items to balance the budget. Again, that is the discipline needed to make the process work.

Let's talk about the pros and cons of this budget method as opposed to the more traditional methods which involve detailed monitoring of each expense item and transferring amounts from the checking account to the expense sheets to monitor each expense item. The pros of the checkbook balance method I use is that once set up it is simple to monitor. You simply monitor your checkbook balance. The simplicity is the main reason I switched to this method. In counseling, I found that using the expense sheet was complicated and confusing for people. Thus, they would end up quitting the budget and thwarting their financial future. That was a shame. So, I really thought about how I could make the budget process simpler to have a better success rate of people actually following through on budgeting and reaching their financial goals. I have found this method, mostly due to the simplicity, to be a good compromise.

The cons of this method are the pros of the expense account monitoring method. Although not simple, it does more accurately track each individual expense item. This is valuable since you can tell very quickly which accounts you have overspent and adjust right away to revise your budget. It also allows you to more easily use a credit card, since each account is being tracked. However, the use of the credit card is a complexity since you must look at each expenditure from the card and then transfer that amount to the individual expense sheet. That is very time-consuming. In the end, most people do not have the discipline, time, and perseverance to use this method. Therefore, by default, the checkbook balance method is the winner.

I also need to talk about the problem of cash flow. That is, let's say you get paid twice per month. Well, your first paycheck may be almost gone after you pay your mortgage and car payment, so how will you pay your other bills? This used to be a source of complexity for anyone setting up a budget. However, since most creditors allow you to choose your monthly payment date, this problem no longer exists. You will simply pay only your mortgage during the first week of the month. The utilities, car insurance and payments, and any other fixed expenses will be paid out during the last two weeks of the month.

At this point, it is a good idea to talk about setting up the emergency fund as part of your budget. This amount can reside in your savings account, but I recommend that it be locked away in an additional savings account. This fund is vitally important to keep your budget from unraveling and give you peace of mind for the unplanned, unexpected expenses that happen to all of us. That is why I strive to budget for even the unexpected, such as putting in amounts for maintenance of the home and car and some amount for replacement of the car since it is a depreciating asset. It is recommended that you have 3 to 6 months of essential expenses in your emergency fund. By essential expenses, we mean food, housing, utilities, and transportation: those expenses you absolutely need to pay even if you lost a job. Looking at our example, these amount to around $2700. So, 3 to 6 months would be between $8,000 and $16,000. How do you choose between those amounts? I usually ask folks to assess the risk of losing your job and, based on that assessment, choose the size of the emergency fund.

I cannot stress enough the importance of this fund. It is the ultimate cushion for anything financially unexpected in your life. I tell people to draw on this fund only if the expense is truly an emergency. If your telephone bill goes up or the utilities increase, even by a lot, that is not an emergency. For normal budget increases, your budget must be revised. Once your budget is filled out, that doesn't mean it is static. The budget is a living document and must be revised whenever your fixed expenses change or your income changes. The emergency fund is a great stress reliever. You may ask, where will we get the money for this fund? Take it from savings, suspend your 401k for a short while, get a second job, have a garage sale; do whatever it takes. But make it a priority and get it done.

A few remaining helpful hints. When setting up your budget, you need to arrange your investment allocation in a way that maximizes your employer's retirement plan benefits. For example, let's say your employer's 401k plan gives you a 3% match for the first 5% of gross income that the employee contributes. In Bob's case, that would be $300 (5% of $6,000). So, we want to ensure we put in at least $300 so we can get that 3% match from Bob's employer which is free money. We all love free money. We could take the other $200 (remember, we allocated $500 to investments in the budget) and put it in the 401k, or set up a Roth IRA and put it in there, if eligible; or just put it in a taxable account. You would have to talk to your financial advisor about that decision.

Another item is spending traps and how to avoid them. I have found in counseling that it is wise to set a spending limit where if you exceed that amount you will talk it over with your spouse or some trusted advisor before you make any expenditure that is outside your budget. That will keep you from making those unwise, spur of the moment, spending-spree expenditures that can derail your budget. Oftentimes folks will set up two limits; one for everyday expenses and one for major purchases such as buying a car, home, boat, etc. The everyday limit is for usual and normal expenses and may be as low as $200. The one for major purchases just states that we will sleep on any decision and examine our budget to see how it will affect the budget long term. I strongly advocate that for major purchases, you delay the expenditure until you have saved up the money and can pay cash. This way, the effect on the budget is minimized except for any long-term use of those funds for retirement or college. There is another side benefit that results from delaying until you can pay cash. I have often seen couples decide that after some thought, they really don't need that item. It gives you time to see how important that purchase really is.

Lastly, you should always keep a proper perspective on budgeting and spending. It is OK to have some fun and not to be too restrictive while you budget. Long-term thinking is necessary; however, it is fine to indulge in some short-term luxuries while you are planning and saving long term. In fact, I believe it is healthy and necessary to go out on dates and have the normal fun expenditures as a reward for your financial discipline. Just ensure to put it in the budget! I will add here that as a practical matter, there are many fun things you can do that are very enjoyable and cost very little. In the end, just being together is a reward in and of itself. In our society, we often equate having fun with spending money on lavish vacations, only to find out that we really didn't have that much fun; it was too much like work. My son takes his large family on hikes almost daily. It keeps them fit and together and they like it a lot. The cost: some gas to get to the park; almost nothing. As they say, the best things in life are free. Very true.

It is important to formulate long-term goals to understand why you are budgeting and guide your decisions as you develop financial discipline. Initially, when you start budgeting, your goals will necessarily be short-term. Develop a written budget, get out of debt, save for an emergency fund, and the like. As you accomplish those short-term goals, you will then be thinking further out, such as college funds for the kids, giving to charities, retirement, and the like. You should sit down with your spouse and your financial advisor to discuss these common goals and explore goals you may not have even thought about. I often have seen that these sessions, if handled properly, will strengthen a marriage and will reveal things you didn't know about your spouse and even yourself as you dream your dreams. It's also a chance to dream big dreams that will motivate you to improve your financial discipline. It will also give you the motivation to get your financial house in order.

God knows that money is a powerful motivating force in our life. That's why He warned that the love of money is the root of all evil. Notice it's not the money, but the **love** of money that becomes the problem. There is much in the Bible that talks about the proper use of money. Part of that process is to become good stewards of what God has given you. The first and most important part is to recognize and believe that everything you have is from God. You will always manage someone else's money more carefully than your own. So, believing that everything you have is from God is a sobering thought that motivates us to carefully manage what we have been given. Ultimately, our final goal is to please God in all areas of our lives, including our finances.

Investing

I conclude this chapter with some investment ideas. I must include the usual disclaimer. I am not a financial advisor. I am giving these general ideas as my own opinions on how to invest. You should always run any ideas you get from any source past a trained financial advisor with the appropriate degrees and expertise. When doing budget counseling, the subject of investing naturally comes up. I restrict my advice to general concepts rather than specifics and always inform them to have a trained financial advisor give investing specifics. With that disclaimer in mind, I feel it is important to pass on what I have learned over many years to help you avoid some of the mistakes I made.

Picking an investment advisor is beyond the scope of this book. However, there is much good advice on the internet. Furthermore, such investing giants as Vanguard, Fidelity, and Schwab have investor education programs that are very informative. As you start your investing journey, your amounts will be small, and if you are not interested in doing your own investing, it is often best to ask trusted friends for recommendations on investment advisors and/or firms. Another source I will often advise is the Certified Kingdom Advisor (CKA). This is a person trained in budgeting and investing and can be found on moneywise.org. You can usually locate a CKA in your area. If the CKA in your area is not trained in investing, he may be a trusted source to find a qualified investment advisor.

Even if you are not doing your own investing, you should be somewhat familiar with investing basics since it is your hard-earned money that is being invested. You want to understand fully what the advisor is investing in and why he is using certain vehicles. Also, choose an advisor that listens well and explains well and that you get along with and will take your criticism well. These factors are more important than rates of return since past performance is no guarantee of future success.

The two most important factors in deciding how to invest are your time horizon and your risk tolerance. Time horizon is when you need the money for the various purposes it was intended. Generally, if you will be using the money in three years or less, the fund should be invested in cash or cash equivalents such as short-term treasury bonds or CDs. So, for money in your emergency fund, that money should be put into cash equivalents, since you want it readily available should the need arise, and you don't want it to be eroded if you put it in riskier asset classes. However, money in an IRA or 401k can be put in more aggressive and longer-term assets, since that money is ostensibly for retirement or college, which is over 15 years out for most of us just starting a budget.

Let's talk about the three major categories of assets. First, the most conservative, cash and cash equivalents, consist of short-term bonds, money market funds, and CDs. Second, bonds are monies, in effect, lent by you to corporations or institutions which pay interest. These are in the middle in terms of risk, between cash and stocks. Third, stock represents an equity stake in a corporation and is the most aggressive with the highest risk and reward. There are also the riskier asset categories consisting of real estate and commodities such as gold and silver. Since these are very risky and generally for the more advanced investor, I recommend avoiding these categories. A CKA or other investment advisor can explain these high-risk assets and include them in your portfolio if you are comfortable with them. In any event, these assets should comprise a relatively small part of your total portfolio.

Next, our personal risk tolerance should be assessed. There are many online questionnaires that can be filled out to give you a rough approximation of your risk tolerance. Further, Vanguard has a questionnaire they use to determine personal risk. The questions typically focus on your tolerance for incurring a loss on an investment. It is a truism that with more reward comes more risk. So, generally, cash equivalents can return about 1 to 2%, with almost no risk of loss. Bonds generally can return around 5 to 6% with a potential loss of 2 to 3%. Stocks can return 8 to 10% with a risk of loss of around 10% or higher. A general rule of thumb is that in a 401k or IRA you should put 40% in bonds and 60% in stocks. However, if you are personally risk-averse, you would want to increase your bond percentage and decrease stocks. Likewise, if you can tolerate more risk in hopes of a greater return, you might increase your stocks to 80%. Those are the basics.

What to invest in. Well, for the novice, I would strongly recommend index funds as they represent a broad index of assets and provide good diversification at a low cost. Warren Buffet famously claimed that the best strategy for a novice who didn't want to pay attention to investing would be to put 30% in short-term treasury bonds and 70% in the S&P stock index. Of course, you could change the percentages to match your risk tolerance. And Warren Buffet is no slouch when it comes to investing!

There is much more to be said on this subject but that is beyond the scope of this book. I have given an overview here for novice investors. If you have an interest in investing, I would encourage you to read books on the subject as there are many out there. Three of my favorites are *The Intelligent Investor* (Benjamin Graham); *One Up on Wall Street* (Peter Lynch); and *The Little Book of Common Sense Investing* (John C. Bogle). Also, discussing investing with an experienced counselor can provide much to your knowledge base. As you become more proficient, you will be able to effectively utilize and challenge your investment advisor and craft a plan best for your situation. After all, it's your money and you are responsible for the results, not the advisor.

2.
Preserving and Directing Wealth

Preserving and Directing Wealth

OK, we have our budget set up, and we are watching our checkbook balance dutifully. With our budget employed, we are assured that we are not overspending, while at the same time, properly saving and investing for the future. And, as an additional bonus, we have saved $10,000 for an emergency fund which gives us peace of mind and also ensures that we will stay within our budget even if unexpected expenses arise. Congratulations; you should pat yourself on the back because you have accomplished some very important goals, namely, getting educated, getting a good job, getting on a budget, and saving for an emergency fund. These are important first steps to securing your financial future. Now, we need to talk about preserving your wealth in the face of life's inevitable obstacles.

The first thing we must do is to establish goals together and plan to regularly revisit those goals and revise them if necessary. The reason we set up goals is to give direction to our financial planning. Once we are saving and investing regularly through the budget, we need to give direction and purpose to those monies invested. If we don't have an ultimate purpose for the monies invested there is really no point in saving any money.

Let's look at some common goals that families establish. To become debt-free is a common goal and it is the number 1 reason people come to a counselor. We will talk about this in detail later on. Another goal is to save for retirement. Indeed, this one is ingrained in our society. That's why we have IRAs, 401ks, and the like. These are tax-advantaged accounts typically for saving for retirement. When we get into our 50s and 60s, inevitably we start thinking and dreaming about retirement. Hopefully, we began our financial planning for retirement much earlier so the process will not be unfamiliar and daunting. Even so, it is better to plan late than not at all. And there are ways to accelerate savings for retirement even in your 50s. So, take heart and start as early as you can. As we discussed earlier, ensure you take advantage of any employer match with a company 401k, as this will accelerate your retirement savings.

Evaluating Expenses

Before we get to those goals, we need to focus on preserving our wealth. To ensure the preservation of wealth, it is necessary to stay on your budget long-term and be ready to make adjustments along the way as the facts change. And for certain, the facts will change, sometimes even monthly. There are unexpected expenses, salary raises and decreases, new expenses that arise, and changes in investment rates of return, to name a few. What it takes to stay focused on the budget is a belief it will work, even when things seem out of control. I am saddened to say that many of my counselees have fallen away when things got tough. On the other hand, I have seen these principles work just as intended for those who are willing to stick it out, no matter what comes. Generally, I would say that once you are on a budget for 12 months, it becomes an ingrained habit and you will likely stay for the long haul. As an encouragement, I know many couples who, once they understand their spending habits and get them under control with the budget, basi-

31

cally put it on autopilot and can focus on other more important matters. Further, it is helpful to remember that the budget is the vehicle that allows you to save for college and retirement. That might help you to retain your focus on staying with your budget.

Let's look at the types of expenditures we should avoid and how to assess each expenditure we are considering. It helps to categorize each expense by whether it is a need, a want, or a luxury. That will help you decide which expense absolutely must stay in the budget and which can possibly be eliminated. Of course, as mentioned throughout this book, both you and your spouse must agree on any course of action regarding spending decisions. Most expenses relating to housing, transportation, food, and utilities are essential and must stay. However, you can reduce these expenses as long as both spouses agree to share the reductions and the attendant inconvenience.

I often tell those I am counseling that it is a good idea, annually (a good new year's resolution, perhaps) to go over your budget and review each budget line to ensure the expenditure is needed or the amount has not gotten too expensive to retain. Many times, this annual review will allow folks to reassess their view on whether the expense is necessary or whether it should be replaced with a lower-cost alternative.

Let me give you some examples to further illustrate my point. The first item in the budget is housing. Couples with a budgeting problem often say, "Downsizing our home may save us so much money that our problem will be solved." However, when you examine the process in more detail, you will find that this is generally not the case. Downsizing rarely saves that much money. This is because, usually, the value of the house they are in is not so extravagant that downsizing will have a substantial effect on their mortgage rate. Even when people downsize, they often find that their smaller house is close to the value of their current house, especially when considering the normal upgrades people will require in order to go through the emotional upheaval to relocate. And because there is substantial hassle and an emotional cost to moving, the savings have to be very substantial to justify such a huge decision. Almost always, once the entire process is discussed, the couple realizes that this is not a wise course of action. Generally, you might end up saving around $100 per month on your mortgage at the end of the process. I do encourage folks to look at refinancing their existing mortgage. This is a process with much less hassle and can net $50 to $100 per month in savings, depending upon the current interest rates.

Other areas to review are the utilities. Generally, gas and electric are the higher-cost items here. It is a good idea to check to see if there are competing utilities to compare costs. In our area, there are several competing gas and electric utilities, and you can choose the one with the longest contract and lowest price. This can save several hundred dollars annually. Also, I have folks examine their TV cable package, including internet, as these costs can be as much as $200 per month. Many younger people have ditched cable and have opted for streaming TV. My son has an HD antenna that gives him all his local channels free of charge. Then he subscribes to Netflix for about $10 per month. That is the ultimate cost savings. I finally decided to switch to streaming TV. I held out until I was pretty sure it worked well and was very user-friendly. I did not want to fool around with an HD antenna but preferred to have a bundled service that included all the local channels. Hulu does this for around $65 per month. YouTube TV is another good choice. However, be warned that to have a good experience with streaming TV, you should have a fairly robust internet speed. In my case, I increased my internet cost by $20 per month in order to get a faster internet speed. At the end of the day, I saved about $50 per month without sacrificing any channels that I really wanted.

You should also examine your cell phone bill. This can be a daunting process; however, the one recommendation I can make is to look closely at your data usage and match that to your plan since the unlimited plans can be pricey. Furthermore, look at using prepaid monthly versus full-service plans, as the latter can be pricey.

Another area is the family vehicles. I generally ensure the vehicles are paid off since cars are a depreciating asset. If not paid off, this will be a priority for budget planning. I will also have families consider whether they need more than one car, like most families have. With many folks working at home these days, sometimes when couples examine their need case, they find that with minimum inconvenience, they can get by with only one car. Obviously, this is not for everyone, so you have to agree on this issue. But if both parties think it workable, this is a huge savings in terms of cash outlay, payments, repairs, insurance, and hassle.

The last item I will mention is your recreation and entertainment. This is an important area and should not be overlooked. I encourage folks to ensure they fund these areas. These areas can be limited for a time while you are saving for the emergency fund or other very important areas, but you must make sure this is funded and used for your own emotional well-being. I have seen many couples ignore this area and, in a few months, abandon their budget altogether because of the emotional strain of being on a strict budget with no fun areas. I encourage folks to look closely at the areas of eating out and vacation. You have to review closely your personal preference regarding these areas and budget accordingly. You also have to devise a vacation that will be fun for you while staying within your budget. As you review this area, you will want to see if you had a good family vacation and if you spent wisely. For eating out, this is very important for most couples, so plan accordingly.

I will next look at the area of insurance. It is a necessary expenditure in our risk-averse society. However, sometimes folks are either notoriously under or over-insured. My job is to get the right balance so that the budget matches the need. Let's first look at the different types of insurance. Life, disability, health, long-term health, home, vehicle, identity protection, mortgage, utility, individual products, and on and on.

Since I am certainly not an expert in this area, I would refer you to an independent agent for advice on what insurance is necessary and at what cost. An independent agent is not tied to any particular insurance company, so, in theory, he should be unbiased in his advice and able to get the best bang for the buck. A good source to find such an agent might be the Dave Ramsey or Moneywise websites. They have search and referral services to help you find qualified professionals.

However, I will give you my experience regarding the pitfalls in this area. In my counseling experience, I have found that most couples are under-insured in the most important areas and sometimes over-insured in some of the least important areas. The important areas are life, disability, health, home, and vehicle insurance. These are the basics everyone should have in their budget to protect their assets and income stream.

Those who are working should have a life insurance policy that has a death benefit of 5 to 10 times the annual salary. This will serve to replace the income of that worker. The younger the worker, the closer to 10 times the salary one should set the death benefit. Oftentimes, life insurance is provided by the employer, but if not, you can get term life insurance at a very low cost. Unfortunately, many folks neglect getting life insurance if not offered by their employer. They mean to get it but just never get around to it. Don't neglect this important area, especially if you have children. Another question is whether you should get term life insurance or buy a more expensive life insurance product that has an investment feature. I believe that term insurance offers the best value and then you should invest the savings according to your more rigorous investing program. This will result in better returns overall.

Disability insurance is another important area, but this insurance can be pricey. For me, since I had an office job and used my mind to make money, I didn't think the cost was worth the remote chance I would ever need the insurance. I would have to be injured so completely that my mind would be damaged. However,

I may not be in the majority on this line of thought. I think if your work demands physical labor, you should definitely consider disability insurance. The cost can be reduced by limiting the percentage of your annual salary covered, and by increasing the wait time before you can collect any insurance proceeds.

Next is health insurance. This topic is clearly beyond the scope of this book and folks should seek professional help in dealing with this important area. However, I will give you some tips that may help navigate this topic. Health insurance is often provided by the employer, but more and more often, due to the cost, the employer has decided to fund only a portion of the cost and pass on an increasing portion to the employee. You should carefully consider the employer's plan and understand how it works for your family. You should also determine if the employer offers multiple plans and which one is most beneficial for your situation regarding coverage and cost. You might also ask your employer if it is possible to reject coverage and receive a cash stipend instead. If this is the case, you might be able to enroll in the Christian sharing plans that are available to folks who have no insurance offered by their employer. The two plans that I am aware of are *Medi-share* and *Christian Healthcare Ministries*. These two plans are not traditional insurance but are recommended sharing plans and have been in existence for many years. They are accepted by most doctors and are relatively low-cost alternatives to traditional health insurance. They both have websites that explain their costs and methods for reimbursement for medical costs.

Let's look at home and vehicle insurance. Generally,

these can be bundled to save money. With home insurance, you want to get replacement value if not cost-prohibitive. You should check to see if floods and other disasters are covered and prepare to pay additional costs to have them covered if that applies to your situation. Remember to shop insurance companies every five years or so, as rates often ramp up automatically and you can save significant money by changing insurance companies. It's a bit of a hassle, but it can be worth the hassle if the savings are 50% or more. You may want to increase your deductibles, as this is another way to save money. However, you should be prepared to have enough money in your emergency fund to handle the increased deductible.

Lastly, we need to discuss long-term care insurance. This is another complicated topic that requires the advice of an independent agent. I did not list it as necessary insurance; however, it is very important as you get older and must be researched and seriously considered. I have not opted for this insurance for myself. It is relatively new to the industry, and when it was first introduced, the product pricing was an unknown. Consequently, many folks who took this insurance soon saw their premiums rise substantially, sometimes 300%. That can take your breath away. Also, the coverage had very high deductibles and many exclusions which, in my opinion, made this insurance not very reliable and therefore not worth the cost. To be fair, the industry has adjusted from those earlier days and the offerings and price are more reliable and stable. However, the time has passed me by to obtain this insurance. If you don't buy it in your 50s, the premiums become very high. I think it is important to discuss the subject of long-term care with your children, as they will bear the burden of this care without insurance. If you don't have children, then it becomes very important to consider this insurance very seriously. There are many costs and options, so there is no reason that you will not be able to find a policy that fits your budget.

In my case, I have talked to my children about this and expressed my desire to stay in my home as long as possible. They have agreed to help me provide folks to come into my home and take care of me and will help with the care themselves. Of course, insurance can cover some of these expenses. You should weigh the costs and benefits of the insurance against the costs of hiring people to come into your home, and you should decide accordingly. For example, my mother-in-law had a strong desire to stay in her home. And we wanted to help her do that. For about six months, we hired people to watch her and we would also watch her and take care of her needs. Hospice also came in to help. There is no cost for hospice, generally. Compared to the premiums she would have paid for 35 plus years, the cost of hiring those people was very small. However, this is just one example, and the illness before death might be for many years rather than a few months. These are risks each one should weigh against the costs. Another important factor is your overall health. If you are healthy, perhaps a high deductible policy with lower costs may be sufficient.

Now, let's turn to specialty insurance, those one-off items for individual purchases where the cashier will ask, "Would you like to insure this $100 item for three years for just $15?" And those endless mail promotion campaigns by the telephone, water, electric, and gas companies that ask us to insure the lines running into our homes for just $2.99 per month. Of course, after the first year the rate skyrockets to $7.99 per month. My advice; stay away from these deals. The rates are very high compared to the cost of the item you are insuring and the coverage exclusions can be tricky and erode the value of the insurance. That's why these deals are marketed so heavily, they offer a great profit to the insurer, and are not a good value to you, the insured.

Another newer boutique offering is identity protection. The jury is out on the value of this product. If you monitor your credit every six months from the three major credit agencies, Experian, Equifax, and TransUnion, then you should be aware of any issues. However, how many people will actually take the time to monitor their credit? Even for myself, I had good intentions to monitor regularly, but after a few years, I stopped. To protect myself, I had my credit information locked so no one can get my credit report. The downside to this is that even I cannot get my report without unlocking it. So, if you are going to get a new credit card or want to borrow money for a purchase, you have to unlock your credit, which is a minor hassle. In the end, I believe this is the best way to protect your identity. And I don't need credit very often so it works well for me. It's fairly easy to lock your credit; you just call all three credit agencies and request that your credit be locked. They will then give you a special PIN to unlock your credit. The other solution is to pay for a credit monitoring service, a monthly charge to continuously monitor your credit reports. Your independent insurance agent should be consulted to obtain the best coverage at the best cost.

Setting and Achieving Goals

The next concept I want to discuss is saving as early in your life as possible. Obviously, if you are in your 30s or 40s or older and reading this book, you may be discouraged, especially when you see the illustrations below that demonstrate the huge advantage of saving early. However, I want to encourage you to reject any discouragement. Getting started on the road to good financial habits is always beneficial, no matter when you start. And passing these habits on to your children should greatly encourage you since they will be able to reap the rewards from saving early.

Here are examples to give you an incentive to start as early as possible. These examples all assume a growth rate of 7 percent, based on the long-term average stock rate of return of 9 percent less the average rate of inflation of 2 percent. Let's take a look at three investors, Barb, Bill, and Bob. Barb starts saving $200 per month at age 25; her savings will grow to over $520,000 by her retirement at age 65. Bill starts saving $200 per month at age 35; his savings will grow to around $245,000 by retirement at age 65. Bob starts saving $200 per month at age 45; his savings will grow to only $100,000 by age 65. This example shows that the first 10 years are so important because of the compounding effect of earning growth. By starting 10 years early, Barb has more than twice as much as Bill by age 65.

Let's look at a 2nd example with Barb and Bill. Barb

again saves $200 per month starting at age 25 but stops at age 35. Her saving will grow to almost $300,000 by age 65. Bill starts saving $200 per month at age 35 and continues until age 65. Yet, even though saving 3 times as much as Barb over his lifetime, he still only accumulates savings of $245,000, less than Barb's $300,000. This dramatically shows the value of starting early. Bill was never able to catch up with Barb's 10-year head start. The only way to offset the head start is to increase your monthly savings rate substantially.

So, my advice is to start saving for retirement as soon as you are employed. Fortunately, most employers have savings vehicles such as 401K plans and IRAs to help you save tax-free for retirement. I encourage the folks I counsel to use these vehicles even before they get on a budget and become debt-free (excluding their home mortgage). It is wise to contribute at least $50 or $100 per month to these plans. Later on, when they get on a budget and become debt-free, the goal would be to put about 10 to 15% of their salary into these tax-deferred savings plans.

Let's talk about reaching the important goal of becoming debt-free. This is a very important early goal of the folks I counsel. This goal is key to preserving wealth, since once you become debt-free, all of the resources you once used to service your debt can now be saved to grow your wealth and satisfy your long-term goals of the college fund and retirement. And for some folks who come into counseling with significant debt, the amount that can be saved and put to work for the future can be equally sizable. I usually run the numbers so that folks can see the potential of their future goals and incentivize them to work hard to become debt-free. Generally, folks who have incurred substantial debt had a lot of fun racking up the debt but soon realize the debt is a burden and a stress carrier. It can often lead to division in the home and even divorce if not handled correctly. I have counseled couples with $300,000 or more in debt and, fortunately, with equally high salaries. Those in this position have the potential to whittle down the debt within 18 to 36 months with the right plan and good discipline to stay on track.

As I discussed in the previous chapter, once an honest assessment is taken regarding necessary expenditures and this is formalized into a budget, the excess income can be used to pay off the debt. I always stress to the couple I am counseling that this always works if the budget is maintained and they really want to use discipline to attack the problem. But both parties have to be on board with the budget and persevere to maintain the budget and stay within spending limits. Generally, once someone is on a budget for six months, they see the debt being reduced, along with the stress, and the relief that it is actually working carries them along to continue the plan.

Of course, the major goals are the same. It's the timing of accomplishing those goals that can be varied depending upon your desires. The short-term goals generally have to be accomplished in a defined order. First, we assess the income and expenses. We then determine how the major expenses can be eliminated or reduced. The budget is planned, written down, and executed. Over the next few weeks and months of execution, revisions are made to make the budget workable. In that same timeframe, the emergency fund is built up from the saving expense line item and other strategies. What are these strategies? Sell some of your junk, have a garage sale, collect pop cans, get a second job; I'm sure you can think of some even better ones. Finally, the excess income is applied to the debt until it is eliminated. During this phase, savings to employer plans may be temporarily suspended, as it is important to reach debt elimination except for the home mortgage. Once the debt is gone, one can begin to work on long-term goals such as paying off the home, college for the kids, retirement, and legacy saving.

Regarding the long-term goals, folks often ask, "In what order should I attack these goals?" Retirement is usually handled automatically, as early as possible, through the employer 401K plan. The usual question is whether to pay off the home early or save for college tuition. If a couple has a strong conviction to be completely debt-free, then that usually takes care of the inquiry. With a strong conviction, the home debt should be eliminated first. If there is no strong conviction, I usually examine their home debt and run numbers to see how much interest will be saved with extra payments. From there, I let the couple decide how much to put on the house payoff. With anything left over, we will apportion that to college funds for the kids. Often, when the budget planning is first started, there is no excess income after retirement savings. However, as income increases over time, these long-term goals can be funded.

The number one question people ask regarding retirement savings is, "How much do I need?" Since you already have a budget and know what you're spending now, that question is much easier to answer. Let's look at Bob and Barb. According to their budget, their monthly need right now is $5000, which includes their giving to charities of $500. Let's assume Bob is 40 years old and Barb is slightly younger (we don't discuss a woman's age unless absolutely forced to). So, let's assume that they will need 90% of today's income, which is $4500, in retirement. You might ask, why 90%? The experts say 75 to 85%. I have found that due to inflation, increased health costs and premiums, and increased traveling in retirement, 90 to 100% is a more realistic and conservatively safe number. We then need to figure out what monthly amount they will get from social security. You can go to bankrate.com and use their calculators or go directly to SSA.gov and input their numbers. Using Bankrate, the monthly amount for Bob and Barb (assuming Barb did not work and will be taking the spousal benefit) is $3400. So, that leaves a monthly need of around $1100 to be supplied by their retirement fund. I will assume that the $500 per month in their budget for investments is put into a Roth IRA. Using the Roth IRA calculator from Bankrate, the fund that accumulates at age 65 when Bob wants to retire is around $329,000. So, will this be enough to retire and fund the $1100 per month needed? Using the Bankrate annuity calculator, the amount needed to fund an $1100 per month withdrawal, assuming a 6% return over 30 years, is around $185,000. So, Bob will comfortably have enough to fund an $1100 per month withdrawal since his Roth IRA account of $329,000 will have well over the $185,000 needed.

At this point, you might ask, "How did you make all

the assumptions needed to use these calculators and compute the retirement fund needed?" Well, it's largely up to you, of course, using recommendations from financial experts. For example, why use a 30-year period for the annuity since this will fund Bob's retirement until he is age 95? That seems excessive since the average age of death in the US is around 80. When making assumptions, it's better to lean on the side of being conservative. That's why I chose an investment rate of return of 6%, rather than 8 to 10%, which is the average for a 60/40 stock/bond investment. And for the annuity calculation, I used a salary increase of 1%, rather than the national average of 2 to 3%. So, all along the way, I have been conservative in my assumptions, since it is better to be surprised on the upside rather than the downside. If you are surprised on the downside, you run out of money before you run out of life; not a good result.

Now let's suppose Bob says to you, "I'm worried about my healthcare premiums being very high in retirement since right now my employer is paying my premiums." Let's put another $400 per month in need to raise his amount needed in retirement from $4500 to $4900. Subtracting his social security of $3400, that would put his need for the Roth IRA at $1500, rather than the original $1100. Using the annuity calculator, the fund needed to fund the $1500 per month withdrawal with the same assumptions is around $252,000. Since that is still less than the $329,000 in his Roth IRA at retirement, he will have enough to fund his retirement. And that emphasizes the beauty of doing the math and using the calculators. You can change your assumptions and recompute the amounts to ensure you are on track and your assumptions are reasonable. This is extremely important as time marches on and your thinking and assumptions, as well as your salary and rate of return on your investments, changes and fluctuates. I recommend you have a financial advisor check your assumptions and math to ensure your computations are sound. You can find fee-based advisors with the major mutual fund companies such as Vanguard, Fidelity, and Schwab, or no-fee advisors from Compass Financial, moneywise.org, or other Christian organizations. Also, your church will likely have some advisors that will check your assumptions.

Another question I get often is "Is it biblical to retire and when is the right age to retire?" Well, the concept of retirement is not really found in the Bible; it's more of a man-made thing. So, if that is the case, as Christians, why are we spending so much time and energy worrying about retirement? Although the Bible does assume that we will be using our time and energy wisely until we die, it does not specify we have to stay in our current employment until we die. So, my advice is while you should stay active in body and mind after you retire, there is an appropriate time to retire from your current job and take up some new form of activity. Mentally and physically, most people get a sense when it is time to retire and take up a new activity and lifestyle that still is productive in your retirement years. And, of course, you want to be financially prepared to take up that new activity. Otherwise, you will be forced to remain in your job long after you are mentally and physically able to perform adequately. Not a good situation for you or your employer. You want to prepare financially, but just as important, you want to think about what you will do that is rewarding and productive in your retirement years. I encourage people to think and plan about what they will do in retirement, long before they retire, at least 12 months before.

I can speak best about this process from my own experience. About one year before I retired, I knew I was financially prepared but needed to think about what my typical day would look like in retirement. What kinds of activities would I pursue that would be productive and fulfilling? I had some hobbies I enjoyed and wanted to continue; those were woodworking and golf. I have many grandchildren so I knew I would devote a day a week with them. I wanted to continue my financial counseling, but this was sporadic so would take no more than a few days a month. And I would continue doing financial work at my church as treasurer and doing tax returns for the elderly in my church. So, I felt like I had plenty to do to fill my time. However, it took many months to arrive at this result.

So, take your time well before retirement to engage in this process. In my situation, I was able to blend my hobbies, my family, and my financial expertise together to fashion a retirement plan for how to spend my days. You need to spend as much time thinking about what you will do in retirement as you did thinking about whether you have the means to retire. I encourage you to do the same. You may find that you want to get a part-time job, paid or volunteer, to fulfill your retirement goals. Maybe start a new hobby or re-engage in an old one. Many prefer to travel to new lands with new adventures. Write a book (look at me). Discuss your plans with your spouse and make sure you are on the same page. It's very important, because there are many studies to suggest that if you retire to the couch, you will likely cut your retirement years in half.

Let me briefly talk about the right age to retire. There really is no magic age. As I mentioned, often people get a sense of when to retire due to mental and physical limitations and just not being able to perform adequately. However, due to the rising cost of medical premiums, 65 is often a desirable target since people can sign up and receive the government medical program, Medicare. This is a good option in terms of coverage and cost. So, for those who would like to retire before 65, you need to plan to have insurance coverage up until age 65. There are a few low-cost medical sharing options such as Medi-share and Christian Healthcare Ministries for you to research. For those who prefer insurance, an independent insurance broker can help with this decision.

Let's tackle another important and often discussed goal: saving for college for the kids. It's a laudable goal, but often parents feel guilty unless they save intending to pay for 100% of the tuition and room and board for their children. I believe this is wrong thinking and puts unnecessary stress on parents. First of all, most of us do not have the means to tackle such an enormous undertaking. If we are talking about private school, the 4-year cost could be in the range of $150,000 per child. And with inflation, the amount in 18 years could be double that. We should realize that this is the highest cost scenario, as many children can go to a community college, get a two-year degree and then finish at a four-year school or go find a job. Some children should not go to college but rather to a trade school. There are many ways to lower the cost of college, and you can't predict the route your child will take. So, in the end, I encourage parents to pick a goal that is realistic for their income and budget and plan to meet that goal. For example, parents can discuss a yearly amount for each child and make that a goal for two or four years. Let's say Bob and Barb pick a yearly amount for each child of $15,000. They want to save for four years of college. So, their total saving will amount to $120,000. They realize that will not cover the complete cost, but it will help each child achieve their goal of going to college.

As a case study of how college costs can differ for each child, let's look at my three sons. My oldest took the traditional route and went to a four-year college right after high school graduation. The cost of his education was around $60,000. With some scholarship money and savings, we were able to cover the cost without any loans. We had a conviction not to let our children take out loans if at all possible. I had school loans from law school and it took ten years to finally pay them off. I didn't want my children saddled with debt upon graduation.

My second son went to the local community college and the costs were very reasonable: around a quarter of the tuition cost and no room and board. Such a deal. To make it even better, he got a position on the student advisory board in student government, and with that position, he received his education tuition-free. He paid for the cost of his books on his own with a part-time job. At the end of his second year, he received a position with General Electric and then received his last two years of education at the expense of GE on their tuition reimbursement program. Many large companies have a reimbursement program to enable their employees to advance their education. So, my second son received a four-year degree at virtually no cost.

Number three went to community college. He had the problem of not really knowing what he wanted to do in life. His brothers helped him in his decision. But I counseled him to figure out what he wanted to do at a lower cost in community college. I have talked to many parents whose children had the same problem, went to a four-year college for a year or two and then dropped out. That is why a community college is a much better option for those students who are not sure about a major or a career when starting college. It is all too common and understandable at such a young age. Anyway, he ended up graduating from a four-year college and saved a substantial amount of money by spending his first two years in a community college. Our local college has many four-year programs where you can earn a four-year degree while attending the community college. A welcome relief to many parents cost-wise.

Regarding college costs and strategies to reduce costs, you have to consider the individual personalities of each of your children. I hear parents say, "Well, my son needs the college experience, that is, to stay in a dorm, meet new friends and learn to live independently." Some children will benefit from the college experience. However, for some others, that experience is neutral or even detrimental. Of course, we can never be sure, but it is important to get your child's input in addition to your own analysis. That analysis should include the costs as well as the perspective of how your child's personality will be enhanced by the experience.

Enough said about that subject. So, let's get back to Bob and Barb. The goal they have chosen is $120,000. When using the Bankrate calculator for investing, we find that to raise $120,000, they will have to put $200 per month into a college savings program, called a 529 plan, for 18 years. We are assuming their two children are ages 1 and 2. If the children are older, you will have to raise the monthly contribution or lower the goal. The investor calculator requires a rate of return of 10% to achieve the goal at $200 per month for 18 years. Thus, we will have to put most of the funds in a stock index, which is more risky but has a greater chance of returning 10%. Also, note that they will have to decrease the amount going into the retirement fund by the $200 being allocated to college. These are the trade-offs parents make to fund both college and retirement. However, they can rerun the numbers for retirement using $300 per month for 18 years and increasing to $600 per month for seven remaining years until they retire. This will comfortably achieve their retirement goals. Using the Bankrate investment calculator, this plan will provide around $258,000 at retirement assuming a 6.5% rate of return. Note that for the last seven years we have raised the contribution from $500 in their budget to $600. The assumption is that this increase will come from raises in salary along the way.

Another question I often get asked is, "Where to put those funds I am saving for the kids' college?" There are basically three vehicles. One is the ever-popular 529 funds set up specifically for college savings, and these are tax-advantaged funds. The one major drawback is that the funds must be used for college expenses. If your child does not go to college, they are taxed when withdrawn. In addition, there is a 10% penalty. Ouch.

Another vehicle is the Roth IRA. You heard me right, the Roth. Even though this is designed for retirement, it can be used to park funds for college. The little-known fact is that all contributions to a Roth can be withdrawn, tax-free, even before you reach age 59-½. The main disadvantage is that you can't withdraw any earnings without being taxed. So, if you can't withdraw the earnings, you have to contribute enough to reach your goals for college funding irrespective of earnings. And as a bonus, those earnings will stay in the Roth to be used for retirement. So, whether your child goes to college or not, these monies do not suffer the limitations of the 529 funds.

A third vehicle is the Coverdell education account. Its limitations are similar to the 529, with an additional limit of $2000 per year per child that you can put in the account. If you are maxed out on your Roth IRA, I usually recommend the 529 plan since it has very high limits on what you can put in the account. You definitely need to run this by your tax and investment advisors, as this is a complicated area and the rules can change yearly.

Obstacles to Wealth Preservation

At this point, I would like to handle some miscellaneous items. First, the emergency fund should be around three to six months of expenses and put in a separate savings account. I strongly advise this so as to avoid the temptation of using the fund for non-emergencies. If the funds are in a separate account, it will take some extra effort to withdraw these funds and that might keep you from using them unless absolutely necessary. Some folks make the mistake of simply adding these funds to the checking account and making a separate accounting for these funds in a ledger. Over time, these funds inevitably dissipate into thin air, much the same way credit card debt slowly accumulates. Very mysterious. I think you see my point.

Another area is the execution of the budget plan. When you are first starting a budget, it seems cumbersome, daunting, and just plain restrictive. I always ask folks to make a three-month commitment to stay on the budget, no matter what. In the first few months, there are many adjustments to accounts since often the amounts put in some line items are unrealistic. Often folks don't really understand what they actually spend in some areas until they are on a budget and actually tracking their spending. After they get through those first few months, folks are used to the process and often exclaim that they are now excited by knowing actually what they can spend and how much they have in excess to apply to paying off debt and going on vacation and other fun things. Their whole attitude changes and they are now happy and relieved to have their financial lives under control.

I hate to stereotype but here is what I generally observe. The wife is stressed out by the growing credit card debt and drags the husband into budget counseling. The husband really does not want to be there but is doing it to help his wife cope. He will just go along and do his own thing when the budget starts. The wife is happy that they are doing something, anything to turn this mess around. She is not happy about a budget since it will restrict her spending and life in general. But she is willing to do anything to stem the tide of the debt, knowing that sooner or later, the tide will break the bank. I convince them the plan will work and if they stick to it for three months, after some budget revisions and time, they will have things under control. They are skeptical but go along. Three months later, with much back and forth, they have actually seen their debt decrease and their spending roughly in line with the budget and are happy with the results and are believers. Unfortunately, many folks don't stick with it for the three to six months it takes to fully implement the habits and discipline and, sadly, drop out of the program. Don't be those folks.

One last item is giving to charities in general and, more specifically, tithing to the church. While it may seem counterproductive to give to your church while you are trying to pay off debt, there is another more important aspect to giving which must be considered. There is something about giving back a portion of what you have earned—call it a spiritual blessing, or a feeling of satisfaction when helping others—that is important and needful even when we are budgeting and trying to justify and minimize every expense. For the Christian, we believe that everything we have belongs to and was given by God. Therefore, we are just giving back a small portion as a thank you and acknowledgment that He owns it all. We are merely stewards of the funds He has given us, and as stewards, we need to be careful of our management. Of course, God doesn't need our money, but the act of giving is an act of obedience and worship back to the giver.

Allow me to be a little preachy here. No one understands the benefits of the act of giving better than God. For He was the greatest giver. John 3:16 describes His greatest gift. *For God loved the world so much that he gave his only Son[a] so that anyone who believes in him shall not perish but have eternal life.* A wise man said, "It was the greatest gift because it met the greatest need, revealed the greatest love, and had the greatest scope and purpose."

Often a Christian will ask me whether he is obliged to tithe or give something while he is budgeting and trying to pay back his debts. I give out some careful guidelines and let the person decide the best course of action. First, God is pleased that, as a steward, you are trying to improve your stewardship by paying off your debts and getting on a spending plan to control your future spending. If you have a strong conviction about giving even while paying off your debts, then you should follow that conviction. But, I believe God honors your heart attitude and doesn't really care about the method or amount. So, I believe that God will honor your intention to suspend giving for a time while you get your financial house in order. Then, at the appropriate time, you can resume your giving while honoring your creditors and your God. But, in the end, the debtor must make the decision and be accountable for the results.

What about the secular person who does not attend a church? I believe the principles are the same. If a person wants to give to a charity and has a conviction about continuing to give, he should follow his conviction. However, I believe suspending giving is reasonable in order to get the finances under control and pay off the creditors. Once this is done, giving can be resumed, even on an increased basis.

Advanced investing

Finally, let's expand on investment ideas for preserving and increasing your wealth. First, let me start with the usual disclaimer. I am not an investment advisor. So, anything I suggest here is just my opinion and anything you do should be checked out with your investment advisor. With that said, let's review what was stated in the last chapter.

I like to keep this as simple as possible while being as useful and helpful as possible. We looked at the two factors that are most impactful regarding investment vehicles: your time horizon and risk tolerance. We also reviewed investment types: cash or cash equivalents, bonds, and stock. We didn't discuss a possible fourth type, that is, commodities such as cryptocurrency, gold, or other precious metals. For a short timeline, we would stick to the least risky cash or cash equivalents, such as money markets, short-term bonds, and short-term treasury bonds. For medium or longer timelines, we would settle on a percentage of all three and maybe even add some commodities as a hedge on a sudden downturn in the market. Depending on your risk tolerance, you would allocate a higher percentage of your assets towards stock and commodities the higher your tolerance.

With all this in mind and with the goal of taking on a little more risk in order to attain a higher return as we preserve our wealth, I propose adding some new exchanged traded funds (ETFs). We are now in a position to compound our return since we have been saving for a few years and have accumulated some wealth. At this point, one possible approach is the following:

- 10 percent in cash
- 20 percent in vanguard total bond fund
- 40 percent in vanguard S&P fund
- 20 percent in ticker symbol ARKK innovation ETF, and;
- 10 percent in ticker symbol GLD ETF.

Of course, these percentages can be adjusted or eliminated to correspond with your risk tolerance and time horizon.

I have added the GLD fund as a hedge against a major correction or recession/depression. Gold often is a counter-mover when a major market downturn occurs. However, investing in gold is a controversial subject and you will find many investment advisors will not recommend this type of asset. So, I will ask you to listen to your investment advisor, do your own research, and make up your mind. As the Bible says, there is wisdom in many counselors.

Another addition is the ARKK ETF. This fund has enjoyed very much success in relatively few years in the market. I believe strongly in the addition of this type of fund, which emphasizes high-risk companies that are innovators in their particular industries and are disrupting their competitors and major industries and technologies. You should research this fund carefully. Their research is open source and is found on Arkfunds.com. They have five innovation platforms and five different funds to represent those platforms. All of the funds are actively managed, and the fees are much more than index funds and in line with what an investment advisor would charge for his services. The funds typically have 35 to 50 companies in their portfolio. The ARKK fund I have mentioned is their flagship fund and has a blended approach, which represents all five of the innovation platforms. More information can be found on their website. As stated before, do your research and consult with your trusted advisor before you invest.

3.
Passing It On

Passing It On

*I*n this section, we will talk about passing on those good financial habits you have learned to your children. There is nothing more important than giving your children the benefits of your successes and failures in the financial area. If done correctly, your children will reap many spiritual and stewardship rewards as they seek to honor God with their resources now and when they are adults.

Financial Education for Children

Many parents, including me, assume their children will learn about money and finances in school. In my day, this was far from the truth. The school system simply had no courses in basic finance, which would include how to get a job, saving money, setting up a bank account, writing checks and balancing your accounts, getting a credit card, and how to handle credit. Today, some schools are tackling these subjects, but a parent can't assume that it is being taught. Even when taught, a parent should be vigilant about reviewing the subject matter in the course. Colleges do have some of these courses, but I am wary of the quality of the content of many of these courses. The one community college course I helped my son with was of very poor quality.

Of course, parents have the primary responsibility to train their children in personal finance, especially during the formative years. In our church, I taught teenagers a course in money management and how to land that first job. I was amazed at how eager teens are to manage their own money and be independent. Probably a teen thing. But I would encourage parents to begin much earlier than the teen years to begin molding their children to understand and apply good money management skills. With an early head start on this training, your children will be much more likely to appreciate the importance of handling money God's way and applying good financial habits throughout their lives.

The first question is: at what age should a parent start teaching his child the basics of money management? This is dependent on the child's maturity and different children will be ready for this topic at different ages. I would suggest you start at age 5, 6 or 7. You know your child best and can best gauge when your child will be ready to benefit from the fundamentals of money management. If you show your child some coins and explain how they are used by mom and dad, and the child seems interested and willing to learn more, then it is probably a good time to start. However, if the child seems bored, then you should not push it. Sometimes a parent, in their zeal to get the child to learn money management, forces the issue, with the result that the child will avoid the subject even years later. So, best to approach the subject gingerly and cautiously and let the feedback from the child cue you to how far you go. I will suggest it's better to try very small bites of this subject at a time and leave them wanting more. With a young child's limited attention span, too little is better than too much.

Pre-Teens

When the child is young, say less than ten years old, I stress to keep the concepts as simple as possible. And then you can expand into more complicated areas as the child progresses. Be sure to ask questions after each session, and for certain, if the child has any questions along the way, that is a prime teaching moment. Spend the time necessary to fully explain and answer the questions and offer the chance for any follow-up questions. Some children will ask many 'why' questions just to hear your response or out of habit. However, some others will remain silent and just trust the parent to deliver honest insight about the subject matter. After some time, you will get pretty good at telling when the child has had enough and it's time to stop or to expand your time when a teaching moment arrives.

To start out, I usually teach about the three uses of money: giving, saving, and spending. I may give them a bank or other storage device to have a place to put the money they accumulate. There are some very elaborate safe-like banks that kids can get that lock to avoid any sneaky siblings. Some Christian booksellers sell banks with three slots with the three uses labeled for easy recognition by the child. I remember buying one of these banks for our kids, and it was a useful reminder of those three uses for money. Then, later on in subsequent lessons, you can explain why we give and to whom we give, why saving is important, and some very basic ideas on goals to achieve an end.

Lastly, why would a parent allow the child to spend freely on whatever he desires (within limits)? That is the fun part that complements the tougher concepts of giving to others and saving for the future. The spending part is the easiest for kids to grasp since it benefits them directly and satisfies their natural desire for material things. This is the concept they will most identify with, but at the same time, it will help them understand the other concepts. It will also give them the incentive to save and give, since while they are doing that, there is the portion that goes to them right now to spend.

Once a quarter or so, you should have a 'spend' day, a time set aside to take the children somewhere to spend what they have accumulated. For myself, we were not too good at setting aside this time to let them enjoy their accomplishments. The time just got away. Don't let that happen to you. It's important to let the kids indulge themselves and get the understanding that there is some material reward for good financial habits. It's amazing what will sink into their psyche one way or another. It seems that kids have a natural affinity for making and spending money. I see this in our grand-kids. So, it should not be too hard setting up a system for chores as long as there are rewards attached.

How should kids earn their money so that we can ex-plain the concept of performing a job for pay and the three uses of money? There are several good ideas out there. Should kids have a set allowance paid each week, or should they have to perform a set of tasks each week to earn that allowance? My son used a hybrid of these two with his kids. Maybe because he wasn't sure which one was correct or would work best. Anyway, his idea was to have a certain set of tasks each week to perform without pay. After those were performed, the child could earn money with certain other tasks. He had a list of their non-pay tasks and extra for-pay tasks listed on the fridge. After each task was performed, the child would place an X by the task to indicate it was done. Dad would then inspect each task for completeness and then award the pay at the end of the week. You could also modify this system to pay a base amount for the mandatory tasks and a higher amount for the extra tasks. The main thing is to use some system to get the kids interested in doing their work and without really knowing it, learning a great deal about managing their money.

With your system up and running, you may hear a lot of complaints or feedback about it. Listen carefully to those complaints. It will be another teaching moment to explain that the parent makes the rules but may be willing to revise those rules if there is a good reason and a respectful appeal is made by the child. So be ready to revise those rules if it makes sense and will provide more incentive for the troops to work and get paid.

So, your system is running, the kids are learning how to work, keep records (or at least, make an X), be honest, give, save and spend. That's really a lot of good stuff going on. Let me discuss the child who doesn't seem motivated by getting paid or spending. It is rare but it happens. Some just crave attention and praise. In that case, you might explain why money is important in our society and offer to give them extra attention and praise while they learn about money. Obviously, you may not say that out loud, but query the child to determine what they really want and try to provide that along with the pay. Also, if you are implementing this system and some members of the family are older now, you have to explain very well what you are trying to accomplish and how it will benefit them. Since they are new to this system, you will want to get their buy-in as the older children can set the pace for the younger ones.

One last thing. It is important to spend a lot of time explaining why you are doing something and make revisions quickly to craft a system that is workable for your kids. One added benefit to taking extra time to teach the oldest child is that the teaching will often be passed down by the oldest to the younger ones. And, trust me, the younger ones always want to do whatever the oldest is interested in and motivated to do.

For me, it was fairly easy to explain the inevitable questions children ask as to the reasons why I was setting up this elaborate system of chores for pay. Basically, the things I was teaching them were in the Bible. I wanted to teach them how money works in our world and how to best honor God with the wealth He has given us. And those teachings are always for our good, not harm. When you really study it out, we are responsible for teaching our children biblical precepts and we will be held accountable by God for whatever we teach them or if we fail to teach them. Likewise, they are accountable to God for their proper response and application of those teachings.

Teenagers

Alright, the kids are getting into their early teens. Time to up our game and give them even more responsibility. This is scary for a parent but you can put controls in place to help them when the inevitable stumbles happen. In what areas can we add additional responsibilities and privileges? At this point, if the child has been a good learner and applying what they have learned, it's time to give them more control over their money.

I will explain to them the purpose of each budget area; giving for others, savings for long-term goals, and spending for short-term wants. I especially dwell on long-term goals by encouraging them to think of an expensive item that they cannot attain with their short-term spending account. And then I will explain to them how to compute how long it will take to have enough money in the long-term savings account. We will also talk about allocating more from the spending to the savings account if the long-term item is important and they want to get it sooner. It's an important lesson on delayed gratification to achieve a long-range result.

At this point, I may convert some of my budget line items for clothing and recreation to the child so they can use those funds for their own purposes. It may only amount to $10 or $15 per month. But it's important to show them that you trust them even with your own resources. It's usually a bigger deal than you think.

When the child is in the middle teens, say 15 to 17, it's time to start treating them like an adult and teaching them advanced concepts of long-term goals, having a written budget, getting a job, and managing their money with limited supervision. They usually like the limited supervision part very much, but don't give them too much rope. It's time to start a written budget and use *your* budget as a guideline for what to put in *their* budget. Items to consider: giving, car, entertainment, clothing, savings, investments, and cash. They may not be ready for some of the higher-end line items, such as cars and investments; however, it is a good time for education on these items and at least to get them thinking about these long-term goals.

So, their first budget will be pretty simple, but the act of writing it down and reconciling the amounts every month will get them ready for advanced budgeting later on. At this point, banking should be a consideration. As long as the parent cosigns, a child can set up a savings and checking account with an ATM and debit card. This is pretty adult stuff but pretty necessary as we get to the next stage of advanced budgeting. Some parents think it is crazy to trust a kid with a debit card. But isn't it better to make their smaller mistakes while under your control when you can correct them relatively painlessly? Also, it's a good idea to have a spending limit of $20 or whatever works for your family, and when they wish to spend over that amount, they have to consult you and get your permission.

Knowing how to use banks, write checks, and balance your accounts is an invaluable skill, one I never was taught until I was self-taught in my early 20s, when I made many costly mistakes. Another option is to use an online bank or digital wallet. I have never used these types of banks, but I understand they are in many ways more convenient than traditional banks. Although as far as online use is concerned, my traditional bank has converted to online use, so I can check my balance anytime online, send payments, and even make deposits without going to the physical bank. But I want to bring it up here for your consideration. I am sure there is much on the internet comparing traditional banks to online banks and the pros and cons of each. One big advantage I know of is that the online banks' interest rates paid on savings accounts are much higher, often 5 to 10 times higher, than traditional banks. So, it's worth considering these options for banking.

When your child is 16 and able to work a real job, I strongly encourage you to consider this option. When they have money coming in that they earned, they will truly begin to take seriously the budgeting and money management skills you have ingrained in them by this time. Working a job instills so many good things in your child; it is worth the effort and sacrifice for a parent to strongly encourage it. Generally, the first job will be one involving menial labor. This will show them how the real world works, that a job is hard work and that maybe going to college to increase their skills to avoid the menial labor jobs will be worth the effort. Don't get me wrong; I have nothing against menial labor. I did a lot of it myself growing up. God honors all labor if done with the right attitude and for His glory. That first job will instill a strong work ethic, understanding the responsibility of being punctual, understanding the hierarchy of the job environment, learning how to get along with people of various backgrounds, and responsibility for money management. It also allows you to teach them how to apply for a job.

Today, there are seldom any personal interviews, as the application process is done entirely online with maybe a phone interview. So, it's important to put the right information on the online job application, as likely this will be the only thing the employer looks at before they hire you. Gone are the days when you walk into the place of business, ask for a job, get a personal interview, and are likely called back within a few days with the decision. The process today can be just as streamlined, but very impersonal. Sitting down with your child to fill out the online application is a must. Otherwise, they are likely to leave out some critical information.

So, your child got his first job and receives his first paycheck. What a proud moment. He's dreaming of what he'll spend it on. But wait, there are some deductions in his pay. He didn't receive the amount he thought by multiplying his hours by the hourly rate. Yes, this is a universal shocker upon receiving your first paycheck. After you get hit with FICA of about 7.65%, an income tax of around 10%, and a state tax of around 3%, you're lucky to get 80% of what you thought you would get. Note that these percentages are rough approximations and will vary according to the state involved and the amount of the paycheck.

This is a good time to explain taxation and how it is a necessary good in any civilized society. After all, it pays for first responders, the military, and many more. You can explain how investments are taxed and especially those employer plans that can set aside money for retirement which will grow tax-free. It's also a good time to review the section on the benefits of saving early so that your child will start even at age 16. Show him those numbers and he may be convinced. If your child is fortunate, his employer will have set up one of those plans so he can participate right now.

Setting Goals

Let's talk about goal setting with your savings. Kids should understand the importance of setting goals and revising them as time goes on. It is a good habit since if we have nothing to shoot for, we'll never hit the target. We will just drift along, spending what we earn and never being wise money managers. You might suggest some goals, but it is wise to let them set as many goals as are reasonable. There really is nothing too big or too small to set as a goal. The idea is having dreams and being able to reach them through careful planning. You also want to show them the math involved in setting goals, so their goals are put into perspective and they can see when they will be achieved as well as how much it costs.

For example, let's say the child wants a new bike. It's the latest dirt bike with dual shock absorbers. Well, first we have to do some online shopping to see exactly what the bike costs. Wow, that was a shocker. It costs $750. Well, maybe we'll start with something smaller. No, he really wants it. Let's do some math and see when he can get it. If he does all his chores and some extra work, he can pocket $25 per week. That comes to about $95 per month, after taking out what he wants to give to his church. That will take him about 8 months to get it. Let's do it. It's October now and he can get the bike in May, just in time for the summer. So, by showing this simple example, it tells the child a lot about planning, timing, and anticipating a purchase or any other goal.

Now each child is different, so we have to expect their goals will be very different from ours and other children. As they set a goal, we have to get them to do the analysis of whether the goal is achievable in a reasonable amount of time, whether the goal is practical and useful, and whether it will honor God and not be a distraction or lead them down a wrong path. All of these things must be considered each time a goal is set. And talking these points over for each goal will get them better able to do the rigorous analysis necessary to achieve a good result.

Let's take another example. Your child got his first job when he was 16 ½. At age 17, he received his learner's permit and wants a car to be used to go to school and work. He has scoured Craigslist, eBay, and used car lots and found a good reliable car for $5,200. Dad has checked it out and it is a good car; reliable and safe. Fortunately, when he first started his job, he was thinking about a car even then and has saved most of his paycheck for that car. He works 15 hours per week and earns $650 per month and his net paycheck is $520. He gives $50 to the church and gives himself $20 in cash for various small items. So, he has saved $450 per month for six months, or $2700. That means he has $2500 left to save, which he can save in less than six months. But then he remembered his grandpa said that he would pay 50 cents on every dollar he saved to purchase a car. So, he received an additional $1350 from grandpa for the $2700 he already saved, which got him within about $1000 of the needed $5200. He will be able to save that in about two months. That's one excited teen! Two points here, this young man had a plan and saved diligently to make that goal happen. Also, it's good to let your relatives know about your savings goals; they might just help you out.

Attitudes about Money

Now we will talk about attitudes and philosophy regarding money and its uses. From a Christian perspective, we believe that God has given us our money. The Bible teaches that the love of money is the root of all evil. This often gets misquoted that money is the root of all evil. But, more telling, it's the love of money, not money itself, that causes evil. Money itself is a tool that we can use for good or ill. However, God is interested in our heart attitude towards money. And in all things, God is looking at our innermost motives, not necessarily our overt actions. We must constantly teach that to our children so they are always examining their motives for what they are doing. We strive to examine our motives even as adults.

So, if we truly believe God has given us all we have, how should we respond? We should first of all be thankful and properly worship Him for what He has freely given. Further, we must be good stewards (managers) by properly budgeting, saving, giving, and spending with proper motives. That's really what this chapter is all about; teaching our children what we have learned about the source of all wisdom and the proper management of what He has given us. It not only includes money but our time and talents. The Bible teaches that we need to redeem our time and not be wasteful with the days we have been given on this earth. Further, we have certain skill sets that we have been entrusted with and we need to ensure we are using those skills for His glory and the furtherance of His kingdom.

These are the deep questions which children might ask:

- "Why are we here?"
- "How did we get here?"
- "What are we supposed to accomplish and why?"

Fortunately, for the Christian, there are plausible answers. We believe God created us for His purpose. We owe the creator our allegiance and worship. Our purpose is to ultimately glorify Him in all we do. Practically speaking, what this looks like in real life should reflect the ideals of a life lived out similar to our ultimate model, Jesus Christ.

Getting back to money management, Jesus said that it is very hard for a rich man to enter the kingdom of God. He stated that it is easier for a camel to go through the eye of a needle, than for a rich man to enter the kingdom of heaven. Why? Because he is trusting his riches rather than looking to God's plan. That's why teaching children not to love money but to love God is so important. And as we are loving Him, we are examining our motives along the way to keep our hearts focused on Him, not the material, worldly things. As the Bible instructs, if any man loves the world, the love of the Father is not in him. Sobering words indeed.

At this point, it may be worthwhile to take a little theological side trip. I believe there are two very pivotal life questions we must answer. And how we answer these questions will determine our worldview, our allegiances, and ultimately our fate. First, where did we come from, that is, were we created by God or by some random acts with time and chance being involved? Second, where do we get our possessions? From God or from our own efforts. As you can see, how we answer these two questions will significantly impact how we order our lives. I will give you some resources at the end of this book to further investigate these questions. It is my hope you will consider them carefully as if your life depends upon it, because, well, it does.

Investing for Teens

Lastly, we will discuss investment ideas for teens. On this topic, it's wise to gauge your audience very carefully. Some teens are very interested in investments, but most are only mildly interested or even bored. So, tailor your discussion to the teens' interest level. For most kids, the basics are all that they will need or assimilate. You need to carefully stick to the essential items they need to have the best success at money management. I would stress the need for investment awareness as it is necessary to increase net worth on excess savings generated by good money management. Then explain the four basic types of investment products and the risk/reward for each type. Further, you will want to talk about time horizon and risk tolerance and how these factors play into investment decisions and rates of return probabilities. Finally, the necessity and methods for finding a good investment advisor should be stressed. That might be all you want to discuss unless they show interest in going deeper.

For those who want to go deeper, there are many books on investing. Moody Publishing is a good place to start. A Google search will unearth hundreds of books on investment topics. And as I have mentioned earlier, the websites of the major investment firms, such as Vanguard, Fidelity, and Schwab have excellent investor materials and courses which explain investment strategies. Make sure you are ready for the many questions your teens will have after they consult these resources.

If I were going to do one thing over, it would be to ensure to find the time to discuss investment ideas with my kids. When they are teens, it's hard to find the time to just sit down with them to talk about anything, much less investment strategy. I would find a 'just the basics' book on investing, make them read it, and then have a discussion about what they learned. I know it's hard for parents to break into a teen's mind, but keep trying; they will at least know you care.

4.
How and When to Transfer Wealth

How and When to Transfer Wealth

*T*his subject is the main reason I tackled this project. I was searching for practical advice on how to transfer wealth to the next generation and charities in line with biblical principles. I found that there was almost no information on this subject from a Christian perspective. I was very surprised to find so little information about such an important subject. There are so many books on investments, budgeting, and money management in general, but precious little regarding wealth transfer for the Christian. There is much out there on traditional estate planning and avoiding probate. But no useful practical advice for the Christian seeking to employ biblical principles to wealth transfer.

My Plan

After I realized that there was little guidance out there, I decided to craft my own plan using biblical principles I had learned in money management. What I discovered upon reflection was that my ideas, which came out of using biblical principles, were much different from traditional estate planning. Since there was such a divergence from the normal, time-tested rules in estate planning, I decided it would be worthwhile to write this book to inform others similarly situated.

Here is how I am situated. I retired a few years ago. Since I had a decent pension and my wife and I both collect social security, I have not had to use any of the funds I had saved for retirement. Because of my age, the Roth IRA was not used extensively as it is today.

Most investment advisors will tell you to put enough

money in your company's 401k to get the matching funds they pay, and then invest all your remaining surplus in Roth IRAs for you and your wife. Even if your wife doesn't work, you still can put in funds for her out of your earnings. Even though you don't get a deduction for the Roth, the fact that everything comes out tax-free once you are 59 ½ and there are no required minimum distributions makes it the better choice over the traditional IRA. The only exception to this is if you are in a very high tax bracket and you expect to be in a much lower tax bracket when you retire. Very few of us.

So, for me, I had most of my retirement savings in a traditional IRA and some money in a Roth IRA. Let's use some hypothetical numbers for our analysis. Let's say I had $750,000 in the traditional IRA and $250,000 in the Roth IRA. But it should be noted that anyone with anywhere from $300,000 to $5 million can fit into this analysis and utilize these concepts. I suspect there are a lot of us baby boomers that fit into this category.

Soon after I retired and settled into my retirement lifestyle, I realized I probably would never need any of the money saved in my IRA funds. Here I sit, with $1 million and not knowing what to do with it. I know, a nice problem to have. Even better, since I really didn't need the money, I started investing more aggressively in the ARK funds I mentioned earlier. To my surprise, my IRAs were growing at a rate of more than 20%, which is 2 to 3 times the rate of the S&P fund. So, my IRAs were growing around $200,000 per year.

What are some things I could do with this fund? We could travel but we're not big on travel. And when we do travel, we visit our grandkids. Our travel budget is more than adequate to handle our annual travel needs. We could invest in real estate. Of course, whenever I consider a large purchase, I take some time to think about whether the investment will be useful for us, the hassle of acquiring and maintenance for the item, and how the item will fit into our lifestyle. Real estate did have some advantages since we live in Ohio and would like to have a warm-weather location. However, whenever we travel south, we rent a nice house and that suits us just fine. The hassle of maintaining two properties did not appeal to us. So, the idea of real estate just did not work for us. It might be a good investment for you. Certainly, real estate is an asset that will appreciate. But we all must weigh the costs and benefits and then decide. For myself, I want to own my things and not have my things own me.

In the end, I decided I would continue my aggressive investment plan for a few more years. And after those few years adjust my percentages to make the plan less aggressive. Perhaps reduce my ARK funds down to 20 or 25%. Then with whatever balances I had in the IRAs, I would start distributing those funds to my heirs and charities over 15 years.

Here is my thought process for how I came up with this plan. Below is a parable in Luke 12 (NIV) that impacted me greatly on how and when to give regarding my unneeded assets:

"The ground of a certain rich man yielded an abundant harvest. [17] He thought to himself, 'What shall I do? I have no place to store my crops.' [18] "Then he said, 'This is what I'll do. I will tear down my barns and build bigger ones, and there I will store my surplus grain. [19] And

I'll say to myself, "You have plenty of grain laid up for many years. Take life easy; eat, drink and be merry." [20] "But God said to him, 'You fool! This very night your life will be demanded from you. Then who will get what you have prepared for yourself?' [21] "This is how it will be with whoever stores up things for themselves but is not rich toward God."

There are so many lessons in these parables. Jesus stated that He used parables to hide the meaning of what He was teaching so that the lessons would be made clear only to those He intended to be part of His kingdom. We are fortunate to have bible commentaries to help us understand parables. Biblegateway.com is a wonderful resource for reading the bible and there is a free Matthew Henry commentary included on this site. I highly recommend it for studying the Bible. Anyway, let's try to unpack this parable.

We notice that the man is blessed to have a large increase due to his abundant harvest. Does he think to thank God for this abundance? No, he contrives to fashion a way to store the increase in bigger barns so that he may take his ease. What does God call him? A fool. Why? Because instead of using his increase for a more kingdom-worthy purpose, he consumed it on himself. This parable does not condemn reasonably saving for the future, but it does condemn greed and hoarding the good increase God has given us.

For myself, these warnings from God are very impactful. I certainly don't want to be considered a fool by my creator. I strive to be considered a wise steward of what He has generously provided. Many of us have substantial sums of wealth in our IRAs. If we have considered our needs and wants, and have come to the place where very little of the money in the IRAs is needed for our future well-being, then it is time to give some of it away and put it in God's kingdom so that it can be used to build up that kingdom.

Appropriate Standards for Who and When

Who should we give this money to, and when to give it out? Those are the questions at hand. The Bible does say that we should leave an inheritance to our children, and those parents who don't provide for their families are worse than unbelievers. So certainly, your children are an important part of your giving plan. One might ask, "How is giving to our children advancing the kingdom of God?" If they are living godly lives, the kingdom will be advanced through their activities and giving. Of course, to ascertain whether they are living godly lives, you, as the giver, should examine their lives and determine whether this is true. Some might argue that it is unfair to give to some children and leave others with less based on their character and belief system. However, we are not asking what is fair using worldly standards, but what is right and just using God's standards.

The parable of the talents in Matthew 25 is instructive on this point. The servant who dug a hole and left his money in the ground was punished by losing his money and that money was given to the other two servants who got a fair rate of return on the money given them. So, based on their management of the money, the little that the unprofitable servant received was taken from him and given to the other two profitable servants. God looks at our character and how we use the valuable time, talent, and money He gives us. And then bases our increase on how faithful we have been to use wisely those items. I believe that is an authority for examining our children and giving our wealth to them based on how they have used what God has given them. Of course, we don't want to be hard-hearted in our giving attitude toward our children, but we do want to be wise and give to those who will likely use it wisely and for God's glory.

As we examine our children, if they are in true need based on something out of their control, then we should seek to satisfy that need through our giving. However, if a child is not living a godly life and not being wise in their money management, then I believe it is wise to consider reducing the amount we give to that child. This is a hard teaching, but I believe it is best, as giving to a child who is not a good money manager is just enabling bad habits and will lead to their ruin in any event, despite your good intentions. So, in the end, I believe it is honoring God to give your wealth unequally to your children as long as it is based on godly standards. Also, you may wish to give a small portion of your wealth to unwise children for a time to see how they handle the money and while you are teaching them the proper standards you expect. Since your children will be adults by the time you retire, this must be handled very delicately. Certainly, we never want to use wealth as a club to intimidate our children but to make them see the importance of good money management for the benefit of their own families.

That brings us to the next question: when we should give out our wealth? I propose that it is better to give out our wealth over many years, perhaps 10 to 15. As you have heard the saying: *do your giving while you're living, so that you're knowing where it's going.* When you give your wealth over an extended period, this will give you time to examine what your children are doing with the money. Also, this will allow you to adjust your plan as the need arises to manage changes that take place in your life as well as your family. I have a comprehensive example below to give you an idea of what this will look like in practice.

Should we give to charities and our church? I think most of us would agree that should be an important part of our giving plan. If our kids are doing well and have good jobs, perhaps you might give less to your kids and what you give might be directed to the grandkids. Depending on the need level of your kids, this will determine and impact the amount we will give to our various charities. I believe this is honoring to the Lord, to ensure our families are taken care of, as was alluded to above.

When we decide to give to any charity, we must carefully examine each charity to ensure they are being wise in their money management; we must know how the charity is being run and what causes they are championing. With smaller organizations, such as a church, you should be able to talk with the leadership and get their financial statements to see what they are spending their money on and what vision the leaders have for the future. If they are not willing to cooperate with you, I would be very reluctant to give them any gift, much less a sizable donation. Even with large organizations, they should be able to give out their financial statements more readily, since they use these to obtain creditworthiness and loans. Also, they should have a website you can use to get a general idea of their vision and leadership roles and backgrounds. If you are giving a sizable gift or even smaller gifts over a long period that add up to a sizable gift, you should be able to meet with some of the leadership to ensure that you are comfortable with your giving decision.

Estate Planning Decisions

How much should I give to my children and charities? That is a question that is often asked and is important. I will give some guidelines to help you make a wise choice, with the understanding there is really no right or wrong answer. Let's say we have a family of four, with two children who are now young adults by the time the parents are retired. Their two children are following the Lord and are good money managers. They have good jobs and are doing well financially. With these facts in mind, I would tend to give the majority of my estate to my children with a smaller minority to the charities of my choice. Maybe 65 to 75% to the children and 25 to 35% to the charities. Here is my reasoning: the kids don't need much of my money, but they have been good money managers, and so giving to them will advance the kingdom. Whatever remains and goes to charities, if properly vetted as I explained above, will obviously advance the kingdom. Of course, I would have a much tougher problem if one or both of my kids were not handling their money well. And I hope to further explain this in the comprehensive example below.

Let's look at the usual and normal ideas for estate

planning. Most people have a will that will distribute all their assets upon their death. So, once the will is made out, people tend to forget about estate planning and go about their lives. Their attorney may have mentioned that you can give up to $15,000 per child per spouse annually, tax-free. And they may sporadically make some gifts to their children. But, let's face it, life is busy and these things typically don't get done. In many families, they may not have prepared a will, although most will prepare one at a bare minimum. Normally, beyond making out a will, nothing more is done on the estate planning front. And if we think about it, this should not be surprising. There is a fairly significant hassle in even preparing a will, much less a trust or other more complicated arrangement. You have to find an attorney, make an appointment, bring many records once you find them, and then sit down and talk about your death. Not a pleasant subject. So, human nature takes over and we do little or nothing. While not trying to be greedy or hoard our wealth, we end up looking like the rich fool building the bigger barns to store his increase.

There is another side of the coin. For fairly wealthy folks, they ensure they hire attorneys to handle their estate planning concerns. They have heard that taxes can take a significant portion of their wealth if there is no planning. However, in their zeal to avoid taxes, they set up various trusts which are extremely complicated and restrictive for their heirs to deal with for many years after their death. This does not seem ideal to me, either. The setting up of such complicated arrangements is often another form of hoarding, that is, trying to control your money and how it is distributed to distant heirs long after your death. We just have trouble giving up what we have worked long and hard to attain. That is why it's so important to remember the one who gave us the increase. Now, don't get me wrong, in the right situation, say if your child is mentally disabled or some similar situation, the setting up of a trust can be a very good idea. However, for the vast majority of us, it's an unnecessary complication.

Let's look at the pros and cons of traditional estate planning vs. my plan of trying to give away as much as is reasonable while you're alive. The main advantage of using the will is that it is simple. You set it up and forget it. Another advantage is that you retain control of your wealth until you die. Since you are retaining all your wealth you are fairly assured you will not out-live your assets, even in the face of very high nursing home costs or rising health care costs. Your beneficiaries have a good idea of what to expect, although they may have a long wait time to receive the assets. There are no performance expectations for the beneficiaries, except that they must outlive you. For charities, there is a certainty of the amount of the bequest, but not when it will be received.

Here are the downsides. There is no thoughtful planning that considers the strengths and weaknesses of the beneficiaries. You miss out on the joy of giving while you are alive, although this could be alleviated by gift-ing to your heirs. Since you set it up and likely forgot it, if circumstances change, they will not be considered in your estate plan. As your wealth increases significant-ly, it is sitting there unproductive while it could be in-vested in the kingdom of God. Giving your beneficiaries significant wealth, all at once, without proper training, could be detrimental to their well-being. When you retain your assets, you avoid helping your beneficiaries and charities in the here and now when they could use the funds most.

For the wealthy giver, there are these benefits:

- Significant tax savings.
- Controlling your money well beyond the grave.
- Setting up performance standards for your beneficiaries that will control their behavior, according to your wishes, after your death.
- Helping your beneficiaries with laudable goals, such as education or general living expenses.

And these negatives:

- Significant administrative costs to hire trustees and fill out tax returns for these trusts.
- Many of the same detriments listed above (I will not list them again here).

The benefits to my plan are as follows: you are weighing the strengths and weaknesses of each beneficiary and planning your giving to reduce the weaknesses while keeping the strengths. Most notably, your giving is done largely while you are alive, so you can adjust your plan as the need arises and circumstances change. While you are giving, you are interacting positively with your beneficiaries which will strengthen your relationships with them as they understand the whys behind your planning. You are not greedily hoarding your assets until death, but rather freely giving them out to help your beneficiaries and strengthen God's kingdom. The giving itself is direct to the beneficiaries and is simple, not accomplished with expensive and complicated trusts weighed down with many instructions and restrictions. You will experience the joy of giving and helping others.

And the downside. This is not a simple plan. There is much planning to determine your needs, what amounts to give to children and charities, and, most important, the communication of your plan to your beneficiaries. However, once set up, the giving of the assets annually is fairly straightforward. Some of your heirs may not like your plan and misconstrue your motives. You should probably expect this to happen. But if your motives are honoring to God, you have to trust that eventually, your children will get it. The good thing is that since you are giving over a long period, your children will have a long time to get it. The rewards can be great if you can help your child get on the right track financially and spiritually. But the risk is that there will be a division in your family. That's why some folks just leave a will and don't discuss it any further. Less risk, less reward. Just like investing.

Finally, there is no guarantee that you will not outlive your assets since you are giving away assets annually and the compounding growth that goes with it. However, since you are giving away a small portion over a long period and retaining a buffer amount, you should be able to adjust to any significant change in circumstances during your lifetime.

I have given you these many pros and cons to give you both sides of the equation. I hope you will study these out and decide what is best for your family. My part is not to convince you which is the right or wrong way but to give you the pertinent information and let you make the decision. A decision coerced and controlled by me is not one you will be satisfied with in the short term or stick with in the long term. In the end, there is no right or wrong answer, and anyone who is taking the time to read this book already has won my admiration by wanting to do the right thing in building, preserving, and transferring their wealth.

We now need to address the amount of financial assets that should remain after the giving period to satisfy the living expenses of the givers. You don't want to be a financial burden on your kids, so you have to be careful to not give everything away during your lifetime in your zeal to benefit others. Financial advisors are always aware of this problem. So, we have to carefully plan to ensure that we do not outlive our assets. There are several things to take into account.

We need to assess our overall health and make our best guess as to what our lifespan will be. The assessment of our health is also important to gauge our necessity for long-term care insurance and what type of health care insurance coverage is necessary. I talked about long-term care insurance earlier, but I want to stress that if you are in your 50s, you should seriously consider this insurance. Your independent insurance agent can advise you as to the best terms for your situation. I would recommend you consider a lower-cost plan that suits your budget. Perhaps in the neighborhood of $200 per day for 36 months, with a 60 day wait period. Ensure the plan allows the flexibility of either spouse using the 36 months. This is a nice feature that serves to cover both of you but only up to a maximum of 36 months, which amounts to a total benefit of $216,000 (36 x 30 x 200). If you don't have this insurance, you should have $200,000 in the IRA to replace the insurance. After the insurance is taken into account, we need to think about our monthly expenses and income.

Once you have been retired for some time, you should have a good idea of what your monthly expenses are as well as your monthly income. If you are not retired yet, you should estimate these expenses with great care, as folks are often surprised at how much they need upon retirement. I usually recommend 90% of your current living expenses. This is on the high side; however, I take into account likely higher health insurance costs and health care costs and additional income for traveling and recreation. In any event, I would recommend you avoid setting up any giving plan until after you are retired, so you have a good idea of your monthly income and expenses in retirement. If you have a substantial amount saved in your IRAs, say more than $3 million, you may begin to start a giving plan before your retirement. You can plan carefully to project your income, expenses, and monthly needs and then make any necessary adjustments to your giving plan once you are retired.

One area that should be estimated carefully is Social Security income. Folks generally underestimate the value of this income stream. If you are retired and receiving Social Security, you know the exact amount. However, for future payments, you have to include the annual cost of living adjustment, which for the past ten years has averaged 1.65%. For those who have not collected yet, you can go on the Social Security Administration's website and use your actual work history to compute a projected monthly benefit at your full retirement age. If you collect early at age 62 you will be penalized roughly 8% per year for early withdrawal. I generally recommend you wait until your full retirement age, which is usually 66 for baby boomers. It is the best way to maximize your benefits. The only reason you would take it early is if you are in very poor health and not expected to live very long or you really need the funds to make ends meet.

Even after you compute your monthly benefit, you should use the cost of living adjustment for any growth projections, since your monthly benefit will increase annually. Folks are often pleasantly surprised to learn they may collect $50,000 to $75,000 annually if both spouses worked. Even if one spouse worked very little, as long as that spouse earned enough quarters to qualify for Social Security, that spouse can collect up to 50% of what the other spouse has earned.

Once you have been retired for several years and presumably living on a budget, you will know precisely what your monthly spending is and what excess income you have at the end of the month. If you have excess expenses at the end of each month, you will have to draw on your IRAs to cover this excess and this will reduce the amount in your IRAs available for giving. You will have to run projections of the withdrawals out for your lifespan and then determine what is remaining for your giving plan.

You should always retain a portion of your IRAs over and above what you will be withdrawing for a cushion in case of any unexpected expenses arising in your later years of life. You need to consider what amount of cushion you and your spouse will feel comfortable with to handle any unexpected expenses or circumstances that will arise in the future. I would suggest an amount between $200,000 and $500,000. This will be your base amount which will be retained and not given away to your children and charities while you are alive. In deciding on this amount, you should consider any life insurance and other assets that would be liquidated after the first spouse dies. As mentioned earlier, you should also consider your overall health and expected lifetime remaining. I trust that the comprehensive example below will give you further guidance on how this base amount will work in a practical exercise.

Lastly, you should remember that once your giving plan is set up, it is a very long-term 10 to 15-year plan. Therefore, you will be adjusting along the way as your circumstances change or the assumptions you made in setting up the plan prove to be incorrect. The annual monitoring of your factual and projection assumptions will allow you to course-correct and stay on track. Then you will be able to accomplish your giving goals while you are alive and adjust these numbers to allow an adequate base amount for your needs. If your projections and assumptions were made conservatively, I would expect there will be very few major adjustments in your plan.

Communication

Let's now discuss communicating your plan with your children and charities. You must take the time to discuss your giving plans and ideas with your children. Although not necessary, it is wise to let charities know of your plans, even though they are subject to change, so that they can do their own budgeting and planning. There are many questions regarding how best to sit down with children and discuss your estate planning. Because of the difficulty discussing these plans, many folks avoid telling their children anything about their planning. This is unfortunate because having their input is important and may change your mind about some of the ways you were implementing your plan.

Let's cover some basic questions. First of all, you should choose an executor and ensure that the individual understands your plans and where the appropriate documents to manage your estate are located. Do you choose an outside executor or one of the children? If everyone gets along pretty well in your family, you may safely choose as executor one of the children who has good money skills. Always get their approval. If there is tension between the siblings, it may be best to choose an independent executor. You may want to run this by the attorney who drafts your will and get his expert advice on choosing your executor.

Do you go over your plans with all your children and their spouses together or separately? I prefer to go over our plans separately. There may be some benefit to getting the group to think and react to your plans, but I think this advantage is outweighed by the candor you will get from each child separately as they view your plans from their personal perspective. How about including their spouses? I recommend not including them. Since they are not directly related to you, their input will have less importance, and they are unlikely to offer it. Further, I believe it is better to have your child explain the plan to their spouse. They are likely to offer any constructive input to their spouse rather than directly to you.

Finally, what to communicate. I don't think it is necessary or helpful to give them specific numbers on your giving plan. I think just a general idea is sufficient. The fact of the matter is that since this plan is a projection into the future for an extended period, you really don't know exactly how the numbers will turn out. This will also serve to eliminate any tension between siblings if you are planning on unequal giving to them. What you do want to stress is your heart attitude about giving and putting the substantial increase that God has given into His kingdom as soon as possible, rather than waiting until you die to transfer your wealth. I think it is wise to communicate the fact that you have observed their stewardship of the assets God has given them and will reward them with a portion of your assets based on that stewardship. Further, you will be observing their stewardship annually and revising your giving in accord with their faithful stewardship. I think it is important to stress to them that God holds you accountable for how you handle the wealth He has provided and that is why you are setting up this giving plan in this manner. Hopefully, they will understand your attitude and accept your wisdom, especially if they see it as coming from God and the Scriptures.

Your children may ask you why giving them your assets is giving into God's kingdom, rather than giving directly to charities. Even if they don't ask, you need to address this issue in your heart as well as to them. First of all, God requires us to leave an inheritance to our family. Not just money, but wisdom and character, courage and strength, and all the other intangibles that make up a sound Christian life. But money is part of it. However, the Bible teaches that a steward should receive assets according to his ability and then based on his wise management of those assets. And as hard as this might be, we sometimes have to withhold things from our children in order to teach them the correct behavior. Our children can be a source of great joy or great pain. I have seen both sides of it. In the end, we do our best to follow God and teach our children and hope the lessons are passed on to the children. It's never too late to teach God's wisdom, even when our children are adults. The things mentioned above should be communicated as best we can. It's important. And finally, most of all, stress that transferring our assets to a child who has demonstrated he is following God and striving to be a good steward is putting those assets in God's kingdom.

Tax Considerations

Lastly, let's discuss tax strategies when dealing with multiple IRA accounts. First, I give you the usual and wise disclosure. Although I am trained as a tax advisor, I do not want to give out specific tax advice to anyone in this book. Everyone's situation is unique and therefore you should seek a qualified tax advisor when getting tax advice regarding your situation. A further point is that the tax laws are always changing so the general information that I give about taxes may not be applicable in the future.

With that said, many of us will have two different types of IRA accounts where our retirement assets are located. Some of our money will be in a traditional IRA and some will be in a Roth IRA. These two IRAs are taxed differently so we need to approach withdrawals from these accounts differently. If we employ the right withdrawal strategies, we can save hundreds of thousands of dollars in taxes. It's worth paying attention to these rules.

Let's use a simple example to illustrate the point. Bob and Barb have saved a total of $1.5 million for retirement. They have been in retirement for a few years and have not needed to withdraw any monies from the IRAs holding their assets. Since the traditional IRA was created in 1974 and the Roth IRA in 1998, they have much more in the traditional IRA. They have $900,000 in the traditional and $600,000 in the Roth. They have decided to start a giving plan for their three children and their church but want to set up a withdrawal plan that will save taxes. As of today, everything that is distributed out of the traditional IRA will be taxed fully to Bob and Barb. Whereas, there is no taxation at all from the monies that are distributed out of the Roth IRA since they are over age 59 ½ and have held the Roth for more than five years. With this in mind, they decide to distribute the monies in the traditional IRA to charities. Monies going directly to charities are not taxed if coming directly from the IRA to the charity. This is deemed a Qualified Charitable Distribution (QCD) under IRS rules and is not taxed to Bob and Barb. It should be noted that you must be age 70½ to use the QCD rules. If you are younger, any distributions, even to charities, will be taxed. I know what you are thinking: who makes up these odd age requirements? Blame it on Congress. So, if you are younger than 70½, you will have to wait to employ this strategy. Of course, you could start distributing out of the Roth IRA to your children at an earlier date.

However, they decided to give about 20% to each of their 3 children and 40% to the charities. Since 60%

of their assets are in the traditional IRA and they only want to contribute 40% to charity, they have to transfer 20% to the Roth to accomplish their goals. You may do a partial conversion annually to transfer amounts from the traditional to the Roth and these amounts will be taxed. However, if you only do a small amount, say $25,000 or $35,000, the tax cost will be minimized since it will likely not push you into a higher tax bracket. In fact, the amount transferred should be planned to ensure the minimum tax, if possible. So, in our example, they have to transfer $300,000 from the traditional IRA to the Roth. If they do this all in one year the tax cost will be substantial. However, if they spread this out over 10 years and transfer around $35,000, this should accomplish their goal. Notice that the transfer will amount to $350,000 which is more than the $300,000 needed. However, this was done as we should assume that there will be investment growth in both IRAs as time goes on. This should approximate our goal and roughly achieve our planned results.

In this way, taxes are minimized as amounts are withdrawn from the IRAs. This is accomplished since all distributions to charities are made from the traditional IRA and not taxed since they are considered QCDs. And all distributions made to the children are made from the Roth IRA and are not taxed due to the tax rules governing the Roth IRA. Any amounts transferred from the traditional to the Roth IRA are taxed, but the taxes are minimized by making them over many years.

Furthermore, all earnings in both accounts have accumulated tax-free and will be distributed with the lowest possible tax cost. This should not be overlooked since the earnings over many years can be substantial. Let's say Bob and Barb contributed $400,000 to their IRAs. That means that the earnings were $1.1 million. If IRAs were not used, they would be taxed around $385,000 on these earnings. However, these earnings escaped taxation in the IRAs. Earnings in the traditional IRA will be taxed when distributed unless a QCD is used. In this example, it is estimated that Bob and Barb will pay taxes of around $50,000 using this withdrawal plan. If the plan was not used, but the QCD rules were used, their taxes would have been around $105,000. If the QCD rules were not used, perhaps because the IRA owner did not give to charities, the taxes paid would be around $315,000. This assumes Bob and Barb are in a 35% tax bracket. The tax savings would be even higher if the distributions would push Bob and Barb into a higher tax bracket. So, in conclusion, you can see the substantial tax savings a proper withdrawal plan can effectuate.

Comprehensive Example

Well, it's time to tackle that comprehensive example I have been alluding to for quite a while. Let's jump right in. Let's look at Bob and Barb again. And let's add two children, John and Jacob. Bob and Barb are in their early 70s and have been retired for a few years now. The kids are in their 40s. Bob and Barb both worked and both have IRAs. The total amounts in traditional IRAs are $1.2 million and the Roth IRAs total $800,000. So, they have total monies saved for retirement of $2 million. Nice.

In their retirement, they have yet to spend any of these

monies saved for retirement. Because of small work pensions and Social Security payments, they are bringing in around $100k per year. They were pleasantly surprised to see that Social Security payments were $70k. The remaining $30k came from their employment pensions. Their lifestyle is such that they are actually saving around $2,000 per month that they are not spending in retirement, which includes gifts to their children, travel, and recreation. They have a long-term care insurance plan that covers the basics in the event they need long-term care. They have Medicare and feel their health care needs are adequately covered. Since they feel comfortable in their financial well-being, they have decided to spend down their retirement assets by giving these assets gradually over 12 years in a giving plan. Why 12 years? Bob and Barb wanted to end their giving period around age 85 and they are about 12 years away.

To set up the giving plan, they first have to decide on the base amount they wish to leave in the IRAs and which IRAs it should be left in. Bob felt comfortable leaving a total base amount of $250,000 and Barb felt comfortable at around $500,000. They consulted a CKA (Certified Kingdom Advisor) in their area they found through the website moneywise.org. The advisor noted that they were in decent health but thought $250,000 was a little low. After the consultation, they decided on $400,000 in total to be left in the traditional IRAs. So that would amount to $200,000 in each IRA. They chose to leave the base amount in the traditional IRAs since they felt it was a fairly remote chance they would have to use it, and if it was for a medical reason, there is an exception to taxation for that purpose. This would allow the Roth IRA to grow unimpeded. Therefore, they would have $800,000 in the traditional IRA to distribute and $800,000 in the Roth IRA.

Now we must consider the annual percentages to be given to charity and the children. To maximize tax savings, they want to use the traditional IRAs to distribute to charities and the Roth IRAs for John and Jacob, as much as possible. Therefore, we will do a calculation to determine how much we should transfer from the traditional IRAs to the Roth IRAs over the 12 years. After the calculation is done, it will not have to be done again since everything left in the traditional IRAs will be transferred to the charities and the two boys will receive everything left in the Roth IRAs. Let's do the calculation to see how this will work.

The first thing Bob and Barb must determine is how much of their total should be given to charities and to the kids. After much thought and prayer, they decide to leave 30% to charities, with the remaining 70% for their kids. Knowing that 30% of the total $1.6 million will go to charities, means that $480,000 should be in the traditional IRA. So, therefore, we will want to transfer $320,000 from the traditional IRA to the Roth IRA to be given to the children. To minimize taxes, we need to transfer this amount over an extended period. So, it is decided to transfer $30,000 per year for 12 years, for a total of $360,000. Note that this amount is more than the $320,000 needed. However, this will offset some of the growth that will occur in the account over the 12 years.

Now that we know what distributions will be coming out of the traditional IRA to the Roth IRA, we can assume a rate of return of 5%. Of course, if you are investing more aggressively you might assume a higher rate of return. We will draw out of the traditional IRA for charities 1/12 the first year, 1/11 the second year, 1/10 the third year, and so on until in the 12th year the fund will be exhausted, except for the $400,000 base amount. Knowing the assumed earnings rate, the $30,000 yearly distribution to the Roth IRA, and the amount distributed to charities, the chart below shows us the balance in the fund over 12 years. I have rounded some numbers for simplicity.

	Base Amount	Remainder	Dist. to Roth IRA	Earnings	Dist. charities	Balance
1	$400,000	$800,000	$30,000	$58,000	$69,000	$1,159,000
2	$400,000	$759,000	$30,000	$56,000	$71,000	$1,114,000
3	$400,000	$714,000	$30,000	$54,000	$74,000	$1,064,000
4	$400,000	$664,000	$30,000	$52,000	$76,000	$1,010,000
5	$400,000	$610,000	$30,000	$49,000	$79,000	$950,000
6	$400,000	$550,000	$30,000	$46,000	$81,000	$885,000
7	$400,000	$485,000	$30,000	$43,000	$83,000	$815,000
8	$400,000	$415,000	$30,000	$39,000	$85,000	$739,000
9	$400,000	$339,000	$30,000	$35,000	$86,000	$658,000
10	$400,000	$258,000	$30,000	$31,000	$86,000	$573,000
11	$400,000	$173,000	$30,000	$27,000	$85,000	$485,000
12	$400,000	$85,000	$30,000	$23,000	$78,000	$400,000

As you can see, after the 12th year, the balance is $400,000. And that equals the base amount we wanted to retain for any unexpected circumstances. The average distribution to charities is around $80,000 while distributing $30,000 each year to the Roth IRA for the boys. The nice thing is that this chart can be put in a spreadsheet and you can then do what-ifs to see how changing earnings or distributions to the Roth will change the numbers. As each year progresses, you can put in the actual earnings in the fund to see how the numbers will progress for the remaining years.

You should congratulate yourselves, since by using this giving plan you have distributed around $80,000 to charities annually and that gave you the ability to see how the charities were using your funds. That way, you can adjust your giving based on the stewardship exhibited by the leadership in those charities. In addition, you benefited by directing those funds according to your wishes on an annual basis. But the main benefit is that you put your money to work in the kingdom of God today instead of letting it sit idle for 12 years. Well done.

All right, now let's look at the Roth IRA and calculate numbers for the boys. First, we need to determine what amounts each boy should receive based on their management of their own money. Well, it turns out, John has been on a budget for many years and has managed his money well. He and his spouse do not live above their means, pay off their credit cards in full every month, and have an emergency fund set aside. They faithfully attend church as well. So, Bob and Barb feel comfortable giving John the full 50% share of the fund.

It's a little more difficult determination for Jacob. He has struggled with money management. He has a decent job but just does not have the perseverance or interest in being on a budget. He has some significant credit card debt and struggles to make ends meet each month. In short, he's not in a good place financially. And spiritually, he has not been faithful in attending church, although he attends sporadically. Bob and Barb have tried to help Jacob financially, but the help just seems to enable him to retain his poor financial management.

After much thought, Bob and Barb decide to explain the giving plan to Jacob and tell him they will give him a partial share of what they wanted to give him. They will give him 30% rather than 50%, but they will not divulge the exact numbers to the boys. They lovingly explain how he needs to be a good manager of what God has provided and get his financial life in order. They condition the giving of the partial share on him attending budget counseling with the CKA they use for their financial planning. Once he is following the advice of the CKA and has his debt under control and is following a monthly budget, he will receive his full share. Jacob agrees with this plan. It takes him three years, but at the end of that time Jacob is on a budget, has his debt under control, and is very happy he followed the advice of the CKA. At that time, Jacob starts receiving his full 50% share of the giving plan.

The chart below will show the fund balance, taking into account the assumed 5% rate of return, the receipt of the $30,000 from the traditional IRA, the full distribution to John, and the partial distribution for the first 3 years to Jacob, followed by the full distribution.

	Beg. balance	Trad. IRA	Earnings	Dist. to John	Dist. to Jacob	End Balance
1	$800,000	$30,000	$42,000	$36,000	$22,000	$814,000
2	$814,000	$30,000	$42,000	$40,000	$24,000	$822,000
3	$822,000	$30,000	$43,000	$45,000	$27,000	$823,000
4	$823,000	$30,000	$43,000	$50,000	$50,000	$796,000
5	$796,000	$30,000	$41,000	$54,000	$54,000	$759,000
6	$759,000	$30,000	$39,000	$59,000	$59,000	$710,000
7	$710,000	$30,000	$37,000	$65,000	$65,000	$647,000

8	$647,000	$30,000	$34,000	$71,000	$71,000	$569,000
9	$569,000	$30,000	$30,000	$79,000	$79,000	$471,000
10	$471,000	$30,000	$25,000	$88,000	$88,000	$350,000
11	$350,000	$30,000	$19,000	$100,000	$100,000	$199,000
12	$199,000	$30,000	$11,000	$120,000	$120,000	$0

It should be noted that the distributions in the later years are significantly higher than in the early years. This is due mainly to the compounding effect of the lower payments to Jacob in the first three years. Even without this compounding, the later payments will be greater but to a lesser extent. If one wanted to even out the distribution, the earlier payments could be increased, or the later payments decreased which would lengthen the payout duration. However, for each year, the actual earnings should be tracked and this could change the distributions as well. In fact, you could change the distributions yearly as you are not bound to follow the model. If in a particular year you don't like the amount of the distribution, it may be increased or decreased and the model will show the attendant results.

Again, this model shows how you can distribute your Roth IRA monies to your kids, tax-free, and get that money into God's kingdom through your children so that it can be used today for His glory. Since this money is distributed over 12 years, there is plenty of time to adjust for any change in circumstances. If some of the money is needed by the parents while it is being distributed, the model can be adjusted to retain whatever monies are needed for them.

Another issue that should be mentioned is that if you implement this plan before you are age 70 ½, you will have to wait until that age to distribute monies out of the traditional IRA to charities to take advantage of the QCD rules. In the meantime, you can start distributions out of the Roth IRA to your children. In addition, you can distribute monies from the traditional IRA to the Roth IRA, as planned, since these distributions would have been taxed in any event. Since you are delaying distributing to charities for a few years, you may want to adjust the amounts being distributed from the traditional IRA to the Roth, to take into account the increased earnings growth in the traditional IRA due to the delay. On the other hand, if you would rather start distributions from both IRAs simultaneously, then you can delay all distributions until you are age 70½.

Some might ask, "This seems pretty complicated; is it worth the effort?" Although the chart and decisions can seem daunting, especially when trying to reduce taxes, the actual decision points are very few. First, you have to choose your base amount, then you have to decide what amount you want to give to charities and your children. After those two decisions, the math takes over to compute both of the charts. Now, I will say that if you decide to give unequally to your children, that can make matters more complicated. But your children will be better for your decision to help them manage their money more effectively.

On a personal note, I have used this plan for a few years now and it has greatly benefited my children. The funds have been used to pay off home mortgages or shorten the payment time, setting up an education fund for the grandkids, home improvements, and increased tithing to the church. This is not an exhaustive list, but we are pleased to see the money helping our children and grandchildren and helping build God's kingdom.

I think it is appropriate to add a note to parents on using this plan and making tough decisions on how to treat their children. These decisions are very hard to make, and we are not perfect parents. But take heart, God is a perfect parent, and yet His children in Israel were often disobedient. So, you should not beat yourself up if your children don't always understand what you are trying to do or teach them. Hopefully, they will see your heart and good intentions and take your decisions well. But if they don't, you have the encouragement that God knows your heart and will reward you accordingly. This is a hard saying, but Jesus said if you do not love me more than your father or mother, or son or daughter, you are not worthy of me. So, we must, as Christians, follow God's teaching in spite of our families' wishes to the contrary. Often the cacophony of the crowd is not full of wisdom, but folly.

5.
The Whys of Transferring Wealth

The Whys of Transferring Wealth

*H*ere we need to discuss why we transfer our wealth and why we do so in the manner described above. Of course, there are many reasons to transfer wealth. First and foremost, for a legacy to show whom you love and want to benefit with your wealth. There are worldly reasons and Godly reasons involved in transferring wealth. You might want to control the behavior of your loved one or a charity. Money can be a powerful motivator, for good and for evil. So, we have to be careful about how we use our money and its effects on behavior. We can have noble intentions, but there may be unintended consequences of our use of money.

These unintended consequences are the main reason why I propose a giving plan that takes place over a long period. As we observe the behavioral consequences from the use of this money, we can adjust our plan to take into account any negative consequences that have occurred as the years unfold. So, we may intend to have a legacy of giving and name recognition of our gifts, but that is not a good reason to give. We should instead always understand that everything we have comes from God and He and He alone should know our gift recipients, as much as possible. Our children will know us, but the charities do not have to be informed.

Legacy Giving

Our legacy should be one of honoring the Lord with our gifts and giving freely out of love. However, we should manage the transfer of our wealth as thoughtfully as we managed the building and preserving of our wealth. A proverb comes to mind: Proverbs 11:24 (NIV), "One person gives freely, yet gains even more, another withholds unduly, yet comes to poverty." Thus, this proves that you can't out-give God. I believe if we transfer our wealth using the concepts in the previous chapter, we will leave a positive legacy for our children. We always need to review our motives for giving so that we have a Godly attitude as we employ our giving plan. We want to positively mold behavior so that it will reflect God's virtue and love. We should never use our giving to coerce behavior or as a tool to get what we want at the cost of injuring a relationship.

Thinking some more about our giving philosophy, I have heard it said that we should practice capitalism outside of the home and socialism in the home. This means that we should treat non-family using capitalist principles and family using socialist principles. Perhaps this is wise. This seems to be the case in practice. With non-family, it is generally pay-for-performance. And with family, we give freely because of the relationship, out of unconditional love. However, the Bible does instruct us to teach our children good money management skills, and if they are not followed, there should be consequences to put them back on track. It is a fine line parents must walk to give freely and withhold when necessary as the Lord instructs. And the corollary seems to prove this out, as the Bible instructs children to obey their parents, that it might go well with them and they live long.

Fostering Relationships

One of the more important reasons for using this plan is to interact with our beneficiaries. Because death is an unpleasant subject, parents often avoid discussing this natural fact and how they will distribute their assets. It's a sad state of affairs when the children are surprised to find out what is being distributed and the method and are left with many serious questions about the motives of the giver. It's sad because with good communication, the motives would have been crystal clear and the positive legacy secured.

Another important side benefit is that this fosters better communication with your spouse which will serve to strengthen your marriage. It is good to plan, but all plans and each step along the way should be discussed with your spouse to ensure that you are both on the same page. There are many important decisions that will affect you and your children and the charities you will donate to, so you have to have those discussions. Some of the things you need to decide are whether to give to the children at all. Perhaps they have great jobs and are doing very well financially. In that case, there is nothing wrong with giving them a much-reduced portion of your wealth. Of course, being of the same mind before you talk to your kids is very important so you don't send mixed messages. There will be compromises along the way, but that will serve to bind you together as you explain your plan to the kids.

You also need to decide on what charities should receive your donations. As stated before, you need to talk with the leaders of any organization you plan on donating to. Find out what their vision is, and how they are implementing that vision today. Make sure you agree with their ministry and that it is truly building God's kingdom. Look at their financial statements or have your

CKA help you with reviewing the statements. When you speak with organization leaders, ask them how much of each dollar donated goes to administrative costs and how much goes to performing the actual ministry of the charity. This is important since some charities are not very good money managers. Comparing the dollars going to ministry with the dollars going to administrative costs is a good gauge of the money management skills of the organization. So, look for charities that spend their money wisely, your church included.

Lastly, you want to carefully discuss with your spouse the base amount you want to retain in your IRAs for your retirement needs. This is important so that you don't give away so much that you become a burden on your kids. You don't want to end up in that position. So, husbands, take care to listen to your wife since in all probability her base amount will be larger than yours. However, you should both listen to each other so you can arrive at a base amount that is not unreasonably high or low. I have given some rough guidelines in the earlier chapter, but you must decide what is comfortable in your specific situation. Fortunately, since your plan will unfold over many years, you can always adjust the base amount and re-run the numbers, if it appears you have estimated too high or low.

Stewardship

When you sit down with your children to discuss your giving plan, I believe it is best to stress your heart regarding what you are trying to accomplish rather than the mechanics of the plan. You want them to understand your philosophy and that you want to honor God in your giving, that God is the source of everything we have, and ultimately you want to put it back into His kingdom. It will be important to let them know that you want to put it back into the kingdom as soon as possible rather than let it sit idle in your IRAs. Also, you believe that giving to them is a very good way to put it back into the kingdom because they have been good stewards of what they have been given. Of course, it will be a tougher conversation if the children have not been good stewards. But in either case, it will be honoring to God.

Indeed, when we are thinking about giving, we have a moral obligation to take care of our family. In the Scriptures, it states that a good man leaves an inheritance to his children. Irrespective of the Scriptures, our society would agree that each man has an obligation of support for his children. So, what does this look like in a practical sense? When your children are young, our responsibilities are much greater and include shelter and food, as well as emotional and spiritual training. When they are adults, our responsibilities are more limited but, as the Scriptures indicate, we should provide advice when appropriate and an inheritance. An inheritance can include not only money but training in proper conduct and character, mostly by modeling this behavior in your life.

If we communicate this giving plan and effectively carry it out, I believe we will be giving an invaluable inheritance to our loved ones. They will understand our motives and our longing to please God and at the same time freely give to them and trusted charities to advance God's kingdom. My hope would be that as they realize the care you have demonstrated in your giving plan, it will yield a bountiful crop of family kindness and wealth. I have found that to be the case in my family. I would quickly add that we are far from perfect and have made many mistakes. However, our children sense our love and care for them and respond accordingly.

I talked about stewardship earlier in this book. The Scriptures refer to the careful management of our time, talent, and resources. Since it is important to God, we must be diligent to carefully manage our money. At our life's end, it should be our desire to hear Him say, "Well done, good and faithful servant." What a feeling that will be if that is our testimony. And I do believe this book will help you properly manage your money when you are building your wealth, and most importantly, wisely transfer the wealth you have accumulated through God's blessing. It is an important reminder that God will hold us accountable for what He has provided. That should be enough impetus for us to manage well what we have been given.

Advancing the kingdom of God is certainly an important reason to manage our wealth with great care. Throughout this book, I have stressed this motive so I won't spend too much time talking about this here. I think for each action you take and each plan you make, you need to get in the habit of thinking about how this will advance God's kingdom, especially when dealing with money and your family, your two most important assets.

In the Lord's prayer, it states, "Your kingdom come, your will be done." Have we ever thought about what this means in a practical sense? When I think about God's kingdom, I envision perpetual light, a sense of belonging and love, righteousness and justice, no crying and no regrets, no death, and the streets of gold! How do we advance that vision? We need to be obedient to God's instructions in the Bible. His will be done. And the best way I know how to do this in relation to money is to manage it well to achieve an increase and pass on that increase to those who are striving to be obedient to God's will. That's why it's so important to watch others who are handling money; are they managing it well and striving to follow God's commands and to do His will? And watch ourselves; while we are managing our own money, are we following His commands and striving to do His will in each step of our money management?

We have all heard the expression, *you can't take it with you.* Yes, that is precisely why we need to transfer it wisely. We have worked and saved very hard to accumulate the wealth in our possession. Of course, we understand it's from God, but while He gave us the abilities and perseverance, we took the initiative and labored to earn that wealth. But, in the end, we know that we cannot keep it beyond the grave. With that knowledge, we should be all the more in earnest that it be transferred to those who will use the same labor and care to ensure that it is used wisely and in keeping with God's will.

In this book, we have taken great care to present a holistic view of money management, one that includes building, preserving, and lastly, transferring that wealth in a systematic way which will ensure it is used wisely and benefits the greatest good. In our early careers, we are involved, to the exclusion of all else, in the raising of our families, the pursuit of our careers, and maintaining our marriage. But it is equally important to spend the time necessary to put our wealth management on a path that will give us the best chance of financial prosperity.

Unfortunately, all too often we plan to get our financial house in order, but life gets in the way and crowds out the best-laid plans. Since this is such an important undertaking, and the earlier we get started saving the better, I have stressed the use of a financial planner such as a CKA or other professional. This planner will give you the help and motivation to set up a budget and savings plan and continue on that path until you have completed the steps necessary to attain financial freedom.

Once you have become debt-free, you will be able to save and invest in order to give to your family and charitable ministries. In addition, you will be able to help your church while you maintain your budget. Many I have counseled sincerely want to help their church but lack the funds, often due to poor money management. Once they are able to eliminate their debt, they can then help others with their excess. And they are very excited when they have the means to do this.

Leaving an Inheritance

Finally, we need to spend some time thinking about the recipients of our wealth. Since we can't give our wealth directly to God, how do we decide who should receive our gifts? As we have said earlier, our children are obvious benefactors, since we are instructed to leave an inheritance to our children. How about our grandchildren? If we really want to bypass our children and give directly to our grandchildren, we must employ a trust or some legal arrangement. I am not in favor of such complexities unless you feel the children are unfit parents. In that case, it may be a wise choice. But in the normal situation, you give to your own children hoping that some of your wealth will, in time, transfer to the grandkids. If you have raised them up in the nurture and admonition of the Lord, as the Bible directs, some of your wealth will likely end up in the hands of the grandkids.

Charities, including your church, are obvious next choices since they are doing the Lord's work, helping the needy, sharing the good news, and otherwise advancing God's kingdom. I think the lion's share of your wealth in excess of what is given to the children should go to your church. As the Bible instructs, those who teach and preach the word of God are worthy of double honor. Your strongest giving conviction should lie with your church. You know the leadership personally. You know of their honesty, integrity, Godly character, and love for their flock. You also know of the financial state of your church, including how they manage their money and what amounts are given for missionaries and ministries such as benevolence, children's programs, adult Bible studies, youth ministry, and other areas. With such extensive knowledge, it is obvious that if their overall ministry is honoring to the Lord, your giving should match the testimony of your church. Granted, no church is perfect and none without problems, but when you examine the overall ministry and teaching and preaching, if you find it honoring to God then you should give accordingly.

Other non-church charitable ministries should also be included, especially to the extent you have benefited from their ministry and/or you resonate with their ministry vision. For example, we give to Moody Bible Ministries. We listen and learn from their many insightful radio broadcasts and programs. They have a worldwide ministry and vision, and since we benefit greatly from that vision, they become an obvious giving choice.

Finally, we need to balance giving to our families and charities. This can be a difficult choice. We must determine as best we can the needs of our own family. If they are in need through no fault of their own, then we must meet that need as it arises as best we can. Beyond that, it generally should be based on how their management of their own funds has honored God. There are very few of us who are in real dire need in this country. Even the poor among us live very well in comparison to those in some other countries. Therefore, I first look at the real need of my family. If they have good jobs and are doing well, then I am more apt to leave a portion for charities. However, if they are doing well but not managing their money well, I am more apt to leave an even greater portion to charities. In any event, I will always leave room for the Lord to work in their hearts and change their attitudes to become good money managers.

In the end, it is something of a balancing act with no hard and fast rules. It's something that you must pray about and consult your spouse and, after much thought, arrive at a solution that you both are comfortable with. It would also be a good idea to get some advice from your CKA to get an outside perspective on this crucial issue. In the comprehensive example, I tried to give a fairly extended set of facts about how the children were handling their money, what their attitudes were, and what their level of need was, and based on all these facts arrive at a percentage to be given to the kids and a remaining percentage to be given to charities. I hope this will provide some guidance as you tackle this tough decision. It's likely one of the hardest decisions you will make as a parent. But if you've made it this far, you will complete the task.

6.
Conclusion

The Wealth of Families

Conclusion

*T*he purpose of this book has been to develop a comprehensive strategy for building, preserving, and transferring your wealth, in a sense, to take you from cradle to grave in your pursuit of excellent financial stewardship that will be pleasing to the Lord. I wonder, how did we do? Well, you, the reader, will be the judge of that, as evidenced by your life changes in response to this book. I truly hope there will be some adjustments in response to the ideas presented here.

Overview

We started with building our wealth. The first step is getting yourself educated and, during this process, discovering how God has wired you, what you're passionate about, what you're good at, and what you're equipped to offer to your community. These personal traits will guide you on what kind of education you need to get the job that suits your skills. In this way, you can be properly trained and be the best employee in your chosen field. This will, in turn, offer the best financial reward and the best job for your skills, one that you will perform well at and excel in your career. Finally, you will be able to advance God's kingdom through this employment that is the best fit for you.

After you are educated and find that perfect job, it is now time to get educated financially. At this point you will be earning good money, perhaps starting a family, and progressing in your career. A lot is going on. I'm tired just thinking about it. It's time to go to money-wise.org and find a good Certified Kingdom Advisor, or

CKA. With you and your spouse working with the CKA, you will be able to set up a budget that will allow you to set up an emergency fund, get debt-free except for your home mortgage, and also start saving for your retirement. Since you are starting early in your life, the compounding effect of your earnings will work hard for you to maximize your savings over the years.

Next, we talk about preserving your wealth. You are living on your budget now and comfortable with your spending plan. It's now time to set up those long-term goals and start taking small steps to implement those goals. First and foremost, you need to be saving for retirement. You should be doing that already through your employer plan. You also want to start a plan for your kids' college. Finally, let's plan to save any excess and pay off our home mortgage so that we can become completely debt-free. The order and timing of these goals will largely depend on your personal conviction about being debt-free and the number and ages of your children. But the most important thing is that you set these goals and have a plan to implement them.

The next item is tithing for the church and giving to other charities. You need to pray on this one and make this a number one priority to honor God, who is the giver of all you have. So, take the time to faithfully consider this item, and talk to your CKA and even your pastor about attitude and amount. Then, when you have prayerfully considered everything, give cheerfully as the Bible instructs.

Finally, we did not want to forget appropriate insurance to protect the assets you have and the goals you intend to reach. That will take the help of an independent insurance agent. Your CKA may be of assistance in finding a qualified agent. It is important to strike the right balance so you are not overinsured or underinsured. Also, you want to get the right coverage and deductibles on each policy and get help regarding what types of policies are necessary and which are optional or should be avoided altogether. Also, take a hard look at long-term care insurance and decide whether it is right for you.

We also discussed some investment ideas. We looked at the five types of investment vehicles: cash or cash equivalents, bonds, stocks, real estate, and commodities. And we gave you a basic idea of how these investment categories should be used for the emergency fund, for the retirement fund, for the college fund, and for any other short-term or long-term purposes. After these basics were discussed, we strongly encouraged the use of a professional investment advisor to craft a detailed plan to fit your risk tolerance and time horizons.

One more point I stressed is that it is never too late to learn about these strategies and implement them. Of course, it is best to start as early as possible since your savings will accumulate faster with the help of compounding. But, at any age, these strategies will help you manage your money wisely instead of your money managing you. And I have found that while people have a sense that a budget will be restrictive and take the fun out of life, the reality is just the opposite. When you have mastered your spending through the use of your budget, you have a sense of freedom, as the stress of not knowing where your money is going is lifted and you will have the money set aside for vacations and fun outings.

Even if you are older when you discover these strategies, you still have the opportunity to pass these money management ideas to your children and grandchildren. This certainly is a wonderful time to pass on ideas that will truly help them in life and will advance God's kingdom as well. We took some time to discuss how best to teach the younger generation what money is, how it is used, and how to manage it properly. Also, it is a great time for them to understand that God is the provider of everything we have and for you to discuss the spiritual aspects of money management.

Education and Planning

We provided some guidance on how to change the focus and strategy of teaching their children as they advance from pre-teens to teenagers. Further, we should give them age-appropriate advice that is simple to follow and show them how to execute the advice in a practical way. We also discussed some steps they could take to set goals and revise plans as circumstances change. We talked about planning tips to reach their savings goals and providing them more challenging tasks as they demonstrate the ability to handle these higher-level tasks. The idea is to eventually get our children to the point of being able to handle their own money management affairs.

Finally, we stressed that teenagers should understand the proper attitudes about money. This is important so that they do not become miserly, hoarders, or spendthrifts, but retain a proper balance regarding money management. We also gave some investment ideas for teens; however, we warned that an investment advisor should be sought out to further explain these difficult concepts. In fact, it would be wise to have the parents' CKA sit down with them to talk about budgeting and investing, to get an independent perspective.

We talked about proper planning and setting of goals to ensure you are successful in your money management. You need to think through the process, step by step, with your goals in mind. Many folks just drift along, spending what they earn and, in the end, becoming a burden on their family. They have a sense that they should be saving some money for the future, but they have no plans, no goals, and no focus to put their common sense into a cohesive plan.

Often, when they come to me for counseling, much of the damage has been done. Because they had no vision for the future, they are in a position of having taken on substantial credit card debt, are stressed out by what they see coming soon, and have no idea how to stem the tide of potential bankruptcy. Even though it is very late in their financial mess, it is never too late to reassess and begin to start good money management practices. We will work through the mess and get it straightened out, but I always remind them it will take planning, patience, and time. If they have the right attitude and perseverance, it can work out well.

That's why it's so important to teach your children about money and budgeting and planning at an early age. Almost always, the folks who come for counseling have had very little training in financial planning and money management. That is why they drift along and they eventually get into trouble. If they had the training when they were young, it is likely they would resort to that discipline before things go too far in the wrong direction.

Once you spend the time to develop an overall plan for money management, then you set your goals to achieve this plan. The common goals are having an emergency fund, getting on a budget, becoming debt-free, saving for retirement, saving for the kids' college, paying off the home mortgage, and giving to your church and charities. This is not an exclusive list but it covers many of the goals people strive to attain.

Since this is such a large list of goals, folks can be overwhelmed and not know where to start. Of course, this is why using a financial advisor and counselor is very important. He will guide you when and where to start each goal and keep you on track. You need to focus on one goal at a time so that you work at it diligently until it is accomplished. Once a goal is accomplished, you will then go to the next one in a logical sequence. That way, you will stay on track and be encouraged as you accomplish each goal along the way to financial freedom.

Even within a particular goal, you can get bogged down and discouraged if it seems like you are not making progress and it is taking too long to get it done. This is where the CKA can encourage you to keep going and provide the necessary steps to get the goal behind you. He will have done this before and has the perspective to ensure you that you are on track, or if you have gotten bogged down on a particular detail, to get you back on track. Some people work well on their own once the framework is laid out. Others need the encouragement and help of the CKA to get through to the goal line. Just know what works for you and follow through with your plans.

You want to think big when you set goals. Shoot for the stars and you just might reach them. But even if you fall short, you will still be better for the journey. You want to set some concrete but realistic numbers and give yourself something to strive for. If you set an easily reached goal, you will likely make it but it might not advance you where you need to be.

For example, let's say your goal is to set up college funds for your three kids. Now, you could set a goal that you will reach for certain in ten years without even factoring in investment returns, just the amount you will be able to save in that ten years. Or, you could stretch yourself and set a goal three times that amount, which will require you to increase the monthly amount you save during that ten-year period and strive for excellent investment returns. The latter goal will require you to get an increase in salary or raise additional funds in some manner and take on more risk in your investment portfolio, but it may be achievable, even though far from certain. You have to weigh all these factors and set a concrete goal. A goal that is too vague or very easily achieved is not worthy to be called a goal.

Finally, with the help of your CKA, set up your goals in a logical sequence so you are not wasting time working on goals that will interfere with the ones you should be working on first. An obvious example: you should not be setting up a college fund before you have any kids and before you have a budget. Without the budget, you have no idea what amounts you have available for the college fund. And without the kids, you don't even know if you will need the college fund.

This is why proper planning is key to financial success. When you are not working with a CKA or other advisor, the steps that seem logical to you may be illogical to achieve your ultimate goal, which is mastering your money to do your will. Many couples who see they are in debt, decide to save more money in order to have a cushion to pay off their debt. But without a budget, they will inevitably incur new debt while they are feeling good about paying off some of the old debt. So, the problem will never be solved. They need to review all their spending and income and reduce their spending so they can maximize paying off their debt. But without the proper sequence, they will frustrate their plans and finally get to the point where they give up. Some will wisely seek counsel at this point. But sadly, some will just quit and may even damage relationships in the process.

Finally, I want to end this chapter on an encouraging note. I have counseled couples and individuals for thirty years. In that time, I have seen this process work whenever it is properly set up and patiently executed. I often ask couples how long it took them to accumulate their debts. They typically respond that it was incurred over many years, perhaps two to five years. Then I will tell them that the program they are embarking on will definitely work, just like it worked for countless other couples. But I caution that they must be willing to follow the plan that they put in place, as it will take them at least as long to get out of debt as it took them to incur the debt.

Sometimes they will say that it was fun getting into debt, at least it was fun having the money and doing the things they did with that money. But, generally, by the time they see me they are stressed out and ready to rid themselves of the problem. Of course, I encourage them that the problem can be solved, but it will take commitment and patience. And away we go.

I can honestly say, for those couples who are diligent and committed, they come out on the other side very happy people and, as an added bonus, debt-free and masters of their money, for the glory of God.

My Salvation Story

One last very important item. I want to speak especially to folks who don't know Jesus or have a personal relationship with Him. Oh, you might have heard about Jesus but for whatever reason, you have never gotten past a casual knowledge about Him.

I hope I have earned the right to talk to you about this subject. It is very personal and life-altering. That's why I take the time to present my story of salvation to you.

I grew up in the Catholic faith. My mother was very religious and encouraged us to attend mass in the local church. I was an altar boy when I was young and enjoyed serving with my friends. I didn't learn much about Jesus in my church. That may have been my fault as I really was not interested in the things of God. I had no concrete beliefs about salvation, the afterlife, or Christian theology.

I was fine with this state of affairs until we had our first child. Then we had a crisis. We had a desire to pass on some religion to our son, but since we had no idea where to start, we just drifted along. We had some neighbors who seemed religious and very committed. They were also very nice people and very kind. Our sons were about seven and six by this time. My wife was really seeking the Lord and trying to figure things out. Finally, she went to our neighbor's pastor. He told her about the apostle Paul, how he persecuted the early Christians, had them killed, and later through a miraculous vision and command from Jesus, became a Christian and was forgiven of his sin. Yes, God can even forgive the murder of His chosen people. Knowing that helped my wife realize she could be forgiven.

Later on, it was explained to her how she could become a true Christian by simply following His command to believe that Jesus was raised from the dead and acknowledge that she had committed sins and ask Jesus to forgive her. This is in Romans 10: 9-10. Also see John 3:16, which Martin Luther called *the gospel in a nutshell*. It says that, "God so loved the world, that he gave his only begotten son, that whoever should believe in him will not perish but will have everlasting life."

My wife came home and told me what happened. And then she stated words I will never forget. She said I don't care if you don't do anything else for me for the rest of your life, but I want you to become a Christian and believe in Jesus and ask Him into your heart. Well, if you could have heard the sincerity in her voice and seen the expression on her face. It just floored me. So, I went upstairs that very night and asked Jesus into my heart.

Later on, it became clearer to me what I did. But at the time, I genuinely came to Jesus by faith alone on the promises in those scriptures, not really understanding fully what I had done. The thing I have pondered and can't really explain is why God chose me to be a Christian. I am nobody special, that's for sure. I have learned that God must choose you and draw you to become one of His chosen. In our flesh, we have no desire to come to God. But when He chooses us, His grace is irresistible. You might question whether we have any free will if God chooses and His choice is irresistible. Well, that is the mystery; we do have free will to reject Him, but those He chooses do not reject Him. Think about that. It's deep, that's all I can say.

So, you might be thinking, *Well that's alright for you, but I'm not sure I buy all this Jesus stuff.* Yeah, I get it. You do have to come by faith. It says in Hebrews, "without faith it is impossible to please God." He provides that faith and He calls you. But if you can listen closely to what I am saying, God may provide that faith and calling to you.

Nowadays, I still have doubts from time to time, as anyone honest will tell you. However, I have studied it out and still believe strongly in my calling and the God who called me. I have studied what many learned Ph.D.s with many accolades say about how we were created. In the end, I firmly believe that someone with intelligence created us.

I would refer you to a Ph.D. (Cambridge) professor who is also a Christian. His name is Stephen C. Meyer. He has written many books about creation science and other topics. You can find him on YouTube and he gives you the science behind Intelligent Design. When you compare it with Darwin's theory of evolution, Darwin looks like an amateur who made his theory out of whole cloth, in my humble opinion. The Bible states over and over that God created us and created the heavens and the earth. Yet, many scientists deny this and try to come up with theories to show that we were created by chemicals coming together in some primordial soup. Does that sound plausible to you? Really? Many people who strive to believe these theories, when you dig down, you realize at the heart of their belief is pride. We don't want to be accountable to a creator, we just want to do our own thing and be accountable to no one.

If you are doubting the reliability of the Bible, you can go to Josh McDowell and study his book called *Evidence that Demands a Verdict*. He's an attorney that set out to disprove Christianity and ended up becoming a strong believer when he examined all the available evidence. It's a very compelling book. But it's a thick one, so ensure you have plenty of time.

If you want a very straightforward, simple look at Christianity and the basic beliefs, go to Gospel.com. It's a very good website. Finally, for an insightful look at the life and teachings of Jesus, review the book by Philip Yancey, *The Jesus I Never Knew*.

I hope these references will help you in your Christian walk and convince you to become a Christian. It's the best decision I ever made.

CPSIA information can be obtained
at www.ICGtesting.com
Printed in the USA
LVHW091424061221
705313LV00028B/733